interchange

FIFTH EDITION

intro A

Student's Book

Jack C. Richards

WITH DIGITAL PACK

CAMBRIDGE
UNIVERSITY PRESS

CAMBRIDGE
UNIVERSITY PRESS & ASSESSMENT

Shaftesbury Road, Cambridge CB2 8EA, United Kingdom

One Liberty Plaza, 20th Floor, New York, NY 10006, USA

477 Williamstown Road, Port Melbourne, VIC 3207, Australia

314–321, 3rd Floor, Plot 3, Splendor Forum, Jasola District Centre, New Delhi – 110025, India

103 Penang Road, #05-06/07, Visioncrest Commercial, Singapore 238467

Torre de los Parques, Colonia Tlacoquemécatl del Valle, Mexico City CP 03200, Mexico

Cambridge University Press & Assessment is a department of the University of Cambridge.

We share the University's mission to contribute to society through the pursuit of education, learning and research at the highest international levels of excellence.

www.cambridge.org
Information on this title: www.cambridge.org/9781009040594

© Cambridge University Press & Assessment 2013, 2017, 2021

First published 2013
Fifth edition 2017
Fifth edition update published 2021

20 19 18 17 16 15 14 13 12 11

Printed in Poland by Opolgraf

A catalogue record for this publication is available from the British Library

ISBN 978-1-009-04041-9 Intro Student's Book with eBook
ISBN 978-1-009-04042-6 Intro Student's Book A with eBook
ISBN 978-1-009-04043-3 Intro Student's Book B with eBook
ISBN 978-1-009-04055-6 Intro Student's Book with Digital Pack
ISBN 978-1-009-04056-3 Intro Student's Book A with Digital Pack
ISBN 978-1-009-04057-0 Intro Student's Book B with Digital Pack
ISBN 978-1-316-62237-7 Intro Workbook
ISBN 978-1-316-62239-1 Intro Workbook A
ISBN 978-1-316-62240-7 Intro Workbook B
ISBN 978-1-108-40605-5 Intro Teacher's Edition
ISBN 978-1-316-62221-6 Intro Class Audio
ISBN 978-1-009-04058-7 Intro Full Contact with Digital Pack
ISBN 978-1-009-04059-4 Intro Full Contact A with Digital Pack
ISBN 978-1-009-04062-4 Intro Full Contact B with Digital Pack
ISBN 978-1-108-40304-7 Presentation Plus Intro

Additional resources for this publication at cambridgeone.org

Informed by teachers

Teachers from all over the world helped develop *Interchange Fifth Edition*. They looked at everything – from the color of the designs to the topics in the conversations – in order to make sure that this course will work in the classroom. We heard from 1,500 teachers in:

- Surveys
- Focus Groups
- In-Depth Reviews

We appreciate the help and input from everyone. In particular, we'd like to give the following people our special thanks:

Jader Franceschi, **Actúa Idiomas,** Bento Gonçalves, Rio Grande do Sul, Brazil

Juliana Dos Santos Voltan Costa, **Actus Idiomas,** São Paulo, Brazil

Ella Osorio, **Angelo State University,** San Angelo, TX, US

Mary Hunter, **Angelo State University,** San Angelo, TX, US

Mario César González, **Angloamericano de Monterrey, SC,** Monterrey, Mexico

Samantha Shipman, **Auburn High School,** Auburn, AL, US

Linda, **Bernick Language School,** Radford, VA, US

Dave Lowrance, **Bethesda University of California,** Yorba Linda, CA, US

Tajbakhsh Hosseini, **Bezmialem Vakif University,** Istanbul, Turkey

Dilek Gercek, **Bil English,** Izmir, Turkey

erkan kolat, **Biruni University, ELT,** Istanbul, Turkey

Nika Gutkowska, **Bluedata International,** New York, NY, US

Daniel Alcocer Gómez, **Cecati 92,** Guadalupe, Nuevo León, Mexico

Samantha Webb, **Central Middle School,** Milton-Freewater, OR, US

Verónica Salgado, **Centro Anglo Americano,** Cuernavaca, Mexico

Ana Rivadeneira Martínez and Georgia P. de Machuca, **Centro de Educación Continua – Universidad Politécnica del Ecuador,** Quito, Ecuador

Anderson Francisco Guimerães Maia, **Centro Cultural Brasil Estados Unidos,** Belém, Brazil

Rosana Mariano, **Centro Paula Souza,** São Paulo, Brazil

Carlos de la Paz Arroyo, Teresa Noemí Parra Alarcón, Gilberto Bastida Gaytan, Manuel Esquivel Román, and Rosa Cepeda Tapia, **Centro Universitario Angloamericano,** Cuernavaca, Morelos, Mexico

Antonio Almeida, **CETEC,** Morelos, Mexico

Cinthia Ferreira, **Cinthia Ferreira Languages Services,** Toronto, ON, Canada

Phil Thomas and Sérgio Sanchez, **CLS Canadian Language School,** São Paulo, Brazil

Celia Concannon, **Cochise College,** Nogales, AZ, US

Maria do Carmo Rocha and CAOP English team, **Colégio Arquidiocesano Ouro Preto – Unidade Cônego Paulo Dilascio,** Ouro Preto, Brazil

Kim Rodriguez, **College of Charleston North,** Charleston, SC, US

Jesús Leza Alvarado, **Coparmex English Institute,** Monterrey, Mexico

John Partain, **Cortazar,** Guanajuato, Mexico

Alexander Palencia Navas, **Cursos de Lenguas, Universidad del Atlántico,** Barranquilla, Colombia

Kenneth Johan Gerardo Steenhuisen Cera, Melfi Osvaldo Guzman Triana, and Carlos Alberto Algarín Jiminez, **Cursos de Lenguas Extranjeras Universidad del Atlantico,** Barranquilla, Colombia

Jane P Kerford, **East Los Angeles College,** Pasadena, CA, US

Daniela, **East Village,** Campinas, São Paulo

Rosalva Camacho Orduño, **Easy English for Groups S.A. de C.V.,** Monterrey, Nuevo León, Mexico

Adonis Gimenez Fusetti, **Easy Way Idiomas,** Ibiúna, Brazil

Eileen Thompson, **Edison Community College,** Piqua, OH, US

Ahminne Handeri O.L Froede, **Englishouse escola de idiomas,** Teófilo Otoni, Brazil

Ana Luz Delgado-Izazola, **Escuela Nacional Preparatoria 5, UNAM,** Mexico City, Mexico

Nancy Alarcón Mendoza, **Facultad de Estudios Superiores Zaragoza, UNAM,** Mexico City, Mexico

Marcilio N. Barros, **Fast English USA,** Campinas, São Paulo, Brazil

Greta Douthat, **FCI Ashland,** Ashland, KY, US

Carlos Lizárraga González, **Grupo Educativo Anglo Americano, S.C.,** Mexico City, Mexico

Hugo Fernando Alcántar Valle, **Instituto Politécnico Nacional, Escuela Superior de Comercio y Administración-Unidad Santotomás, Celex Esca Santo Tomás,** Mexico City, Mexico

Sueli Nascimento, **Instituto Superior de Educação do Rio de Janeiro,** Rio de Janeiro, Brazil

Elsa F Monteverde, **International Academic Services,** Miami, FL, US

Laura Anand, **Irvine Adult School,** Irvine, CA, US

Prof. Marli T. Fernandes (principal) and Prof. Dr. Jefferson J. Fernandes (pedagogue), **Jefferson Idiomass,** São Paulo, Brazil

Herman Bartelen, **Kanda Gaigo Gakuin,** Tokyo, Japan

Cassia Silva, **Key Languages,** Key Biscayne, FL, US

Sister Mary Hope, **Kyoto Notre Dame Joshi Gakuin,** Kyoto, Japan

Nate Freedman, **LAL Language Centres,** Boston, MA, US

Richard Janzen, **Langley Secondary School,** Abbotsford, BC, Canada

Christina Abel Gabardo, **Language House,** Campo Largo, Brazil

Ivonne Castro, **Learn English International,** Cali, Colombia

Julio Cesar Maciel Rodrigues, **Liberty Centro de Línguas,** São Paulo, Brazil

Ann Gibson, **Maynard High School,** Maynard, MA, US

Martin Darling, **Meiji Gakuin Daigaku,** Tokyo, Japan

Dax Thomas, **Meiji Gakuin Daigaku,** Yokohama, Kanagawa, Japan

Derya Budak, **Mevlana University,** Konya, Turkey

B Sullivan, **Miami Valley Career Technical Center International Program,** Dayton, OH, US

Julio Velazquez, **Milo Language Center,** Weston, FL, US

Daiane Siqueira da Silva, Luiz Carlos Buontempo, Marlete Avelina de Oliveira Cunha, Marcos Paulo Segatti, Morgana Eveline de Oliveira, Nadia Lia Gino Alo, and Paul Hyde Budgen, **New Interchange-Escola de Idiomas,** São Paulo, Brazil

Patrícia França Furtado da Costa, Juiz de Fora, Brazil Patricia Servín

Chris Pollard, **North West Regional College SK,** North Battleford, SK, Canada

Olga Amy, **Notre Dame High School,** Red Deer, Canada

Amy Garrett, **Ouachita Baptist University,** Arkadelphia, AR, US

Mervin Curry, **Palm Beach State College,** Boca Raton, FL, US

Julie Barros, **Quality English Studio,** Guarulhos, São Paulo, Brazil

Teodoro González Saldaña and Jesús Monserrrta Mata Franco, **Race Idiomas,** Mexico City, Mexico

Autumn Westphal and Noga La`or, **Rennert International,** New York, NY, US

Antonio Gallo and Javy Palau, **Rigby Idiomas,** Monterrey, Mexico Tatiane Gabriela Sperb do Nascimento, **Right Way,** Igrejinha, Brazil

Mustafa Akgül, **Selahaddin Eyyubi Universitesi,** Diyarbakır, Turkey

James Drury M. Fonseca, **Senac Idiomas Fortaleza,** Fortaleza, Ceara, Brazil

Manoel Fialho S Neto, **Senac – PE,** Recife, Brazil

Jane Imber, **Small World,** Lawrence, KS, US

Tony Torres, **South Texas College,** McAllen, TX, US

Janet Rose, **Tennessee Foreign Language Institute,** College Grove, TN, US

Todd Enslen, **Tohoku University,** Sendai, Miyagi, Japan

Daniel Murray, **Torrance Adult School,** Torrance, CA, US

Juan Manuel Pulido Mendoza, **Universidad del Atlántico,** Barranquilla, Colombia

Juan Carlos Vargas Millán, **Universidad Libre Seccional Cali,** Cali (Valle del Cauca), Colombia

Carmen Cecilia Llanos Ospina, **Universidad Libre Seccional Cali,** Cali, Colombia

Jorge Noriega Zenteno, **Universidad Politécnica del Valle de México,** Estado de México, Mexico

Aimee Natasha Holguin S., **Universidad Politécnica del Valle de México UPVM,** Tultitlàn Estado de México, Mexico

Christian Selene Bernal Barraza, **UPVM Universidad Politécnica del Valle de México,** Ecatepec, Mexico

Lizeth Ramos Acosta, **Universidad Santiago de Cali,** Cali, Colombia

Silvana Dushku, **University of Illinois Champaign,** IL, US

Deirdre McMurtry, **University of Nebraska – Omaha,** Omaha, NE, US

Jason E Mower, **University of Utah,** Salt Lake City, UT, US

Paul Chugg, **Vanguard Taylor Language Institute,** Edmonton, Alberta, Canada

Henry Mulak, **Varsity Tutors,** Los Angeles, CA, US

Shirlei Strucker Calgaro and Hugo Guilherme Karrer, **VIP Centro de Idiomas,** Panambi, Rio Grande do Sul, Brazil

Eleanor Kelly, **Waseda Daigaku Extension Centre,** Tokyo, Japan

Sherry Ashworth, **Wichita State University,** Wichita, KS, US

Laine Bourdene, **William Carey University,** Hattiesburg, MS, US

Serap Aydın, Istanbul, Turkey

Liliana Covino, Guarulhos, Brazil

Yannuarys Jiménez, Barranquilla, Colombia

Juliana Morais Pazzini, Toronto, ON, Canada

Marlon Sanches, Montreal, Canada

Additional content contributed by Kenna Bourke, Inara Couto, Nic Harris, Greg Manin, Ashleigh Martinez, Laura McKenzie, Paul McIntyre, Clara Prado, Lynne Robertson, Mari Vargo, Theo Walker, and Maria Lucia Zaorob.

Plan of Intro Book A

Pronunciation/Listening	Writing/Reading	Interchange Activity
Linked sounds Listening for the spelling of names, phone numbers, and email addresses	Writing a list of names, phone numbers, and email addresses	"Celebrity classmates": Introducing yourself to new people PAGE 114
Plural -s endings Listening for the locations of objects	Writing the locations of objects	"Find the differences": Comparing two pictures of a room PAGE 115
Syllable stress Listening for countries, cities, and languages; listening to descriptions of people	Writing questions requesting personal information	"Let's talk!": Finding out more about your classmates PAGE 118
The letters s and sh Listening for descriptions of clothing and colors	Writing questions about what people are wearing	"Celebrity fashions": Describing celebrities' clothing PAGES 116–117
Rising and falling intonation Listening for times of the day; listening to identify people's actions	Writing times of the day "Message Me!": Reading an online chat between two friends	"What's wrong with this picture?": Describing what's wrong with a picture PAGE 119
Third-person singular -s endings Listening for activities and days of the week	Writing about your weekly routine "What's Your Schedule Like?": Reading about someone's daily schedule	"Class survey": Finding out more about classmates' habits and routines PAGE 120
Words with th Listening to descriptions of homes; listening to people shop for furniture	Writing about your dream home "Unique Hotels": Reading about two interesting hotels	"Find the differences": Comparing two apartments PAGE 121
Reduction of do Listening to people describe their jobs	Writing about jobs "Dream Jobs": Reading about two unusual jobs	"The perfect job": Figuring out what job is right for you PAGE 122

1 What's your name?

▸ Say hello and make introductions
▸ Say good-bye and exchange contact information

1 CONVERSATION My name is Joshua Brown.

A Listen and practice.

Joshua	Hello. My name is Joshua Brown.
Isabella	Hi. My name is Isabella Martins.
Joshua	It's nice to meet you, Isabella.
Isabella	Nice to meet you, too.
Joshua	I'm sorry. What's your last name again?
Isabella	It's Martins.

First names	Last names
↓	↓
Joshua	Brown
Isabella	Martins

B PAIR WORK Introduce yourself to your partner.

2 SNAPSHOT

Listen and practice.

Nicholas Hoult

Names & nicknames

Nicholas (Nick)	Madison (Maddie)	Jennifer (Jen)
Emily (Em)	Joshua (Josh)	Isabella (Izzy)
Michael (Mike)	William (Will)	Elizabeth (Liz)

What are some popular names and nicknames in your country?
Do you have a nickname? What is it?

Jennifer Lawrence

3 GRAMMAR FOCUS

My, your, his, her

What's **your** name?	**My** name's Carlos.	What**'s** = What **is**
What's **his** name?	**His** name's Joshua.	
What's **her** name?	**Her** name's Isabella.	

GRAMMAR PLUS *see page 132*

A Complete the conversations. Use *my*, *your*, *his*, or *her*.

1. A: Hello. What's _____your_____ name?

   B: Hi. _____ name is Carlos.
   What's _____ name?

   A: _____ name is Akina.

2. A: What's _____ name?

   B: _____ name is Ethan.

   A: And what's _____ name?

   B: _____ name is Caroline.

B PAIR WORK Practice the conversations with a partner.

4 SPEAKING Spelling names

A Listen and practice.

A	B	C	D	E	F	G	H	I	J	K	L	M	N	O	P	Q	R	S	T	U	V	W	X	Y	Z
a	b	c	d	e	f	g	h	i	j	k	l	m	n	o	p	q	r	s	t	u	v	w	x	y	z

B CLASS ACTIVITY Listen and practice. Then practice with your own names.
Make a list of your classmates' names.

A: What's your name?
B: My name is Akina Hayashi.
A: Is that A-K-I-N-A?
B: Yes, that's right.
A: How do you spell your last name? H-A-Y-A-S-H-Y?
B: No, it's H-A-Y-A-S-H-I.

My classmates

Akina Hayashi

Ethan Reed

5 LISTENING Your name, please?

How do you spell the names? Listen and check (✓) the correct answers.

1. ☐ Kate
☐ Cate

2. ☐ Erick
☐ Eric

3. ☐ Sophia
☐ Sofia

4. ☐ Zackary
☐ Zachary

6 WORD POWER Titles

▶ **A** Listen and practice.

Miss Kato (single females)	**Ms.** Yong (single or married females)
Mrs. Jones (married females)	**Mr.** Rodriguez (single or married males)

▶ **B** Listen and write the titles.

1. _____ Santos   2. _____ Wilson   3. _____ Park   4. _____ Rossi

7 SPEAKING Saying hello

▶ **A** Listen and practice.

B **CLASS ACTIVITY** Go around the class. Greet your classmates formally (with titles) and informally (without titles).

8 CONVERSATION Are you Andrea Clark?

▶ **A** Listen and practice.

Daniel Excuse me. Are you Andrea Clark?

Sheila No, I'm not. She's over there.

Daniel Oh, I'm sorry.

Lena Matt? This is your book.

Matt Oh, thank you. You're in my math class, right?

Lena Yes, I am. I'm Lena Garza.

Jack Hey, Christy, this is Ben. He's in our history class.

Christy Hi, Ben.

Ben Hi, Christy. Nice to meet you.

B **GROUP WORK** Greet a classmate. Then introduce him or her to another classmate.

"Hey, Eduardo, this is . . ."

9 GRAMMAR FOCUS

▶ **The verb *be***

I'm Lena Garza.	**Are you** Andrea Clark?
You're in my class.	Yes, **I am**. (~~Yes, I'm.~~)
She's over there. (**Andrea is** over there.)	No, **I'm not**.
He's in our class. (**Ben is** in our class.)	
It's Garza. (**My last name is** Garza.)	How **are you**?
	I'm fine, thanks.

I'm = I am
You're = You are
He's = He is
She's = She is
It's = It is

GRAMMAR PLUS *see page 132*

A Complete the conversation with the correct words in parentheses.
Then practice with a partner.

Ben Hello, Christy. How _____are_____ (are / is) you?

Christy _____ (I'm / It's) fine, thanks. _____ (I'm / It's) sorry – what's your name again?

Ben _____ (Is / It's) Ben – Ben Durant.

Christy That's right! Ben, this _____ (is / it's) Joshua Brown. _____ (He's / She's) in our history class.

Ben _____ (I'm / It's) nice to meet you.

Joshua Hi, Ben. I think _____ (I'm / you're) in my English class, too.

Ben Oh, right! Yes, I _____ (am / 'm).

What's your name? **5**

B Complete the conversations. Then practice in groups.

Cara Excuse me. _____Are_____ you Alex Lane?

James No, _____ not. My name _____
James Harris. Alex _____ over there.

Cara Oh, sorry.

Cara _____ you Alex Lane?

Alex Yes, I _____.

Cara Hi. _____ Cara Ruiz.

Alex Oh, _____ in my history class, right?

Cara Yes, I _____.

Alex _____ nice to meet you, Cara.

C **CLASS ACTIVITY** Write your name on a piece of paper.
Put the papers in a bag. Then take a different paper.
Find the other student.

A: Excuse me. Are you Min-ji Cho?

B: No, I'm not. She's over there.

A: Hi. Are you Min-ji Cho?

C: Yes, I am.

10 PRONUNCIATION Linked sounds

▶ Listen and practice. Notice the linked sounds.

I'm͜Isabella.   She's͜over there.   You're͜in my class.

11 SPEAKING Personal information

▶ **A** Listen and practice.

0	1	2	3	4	5	6	7	8	9	10
zero (oh)	one	two	three	four	five	six	seven	eight	nine	ten

▶ **B** **PAIR WORK** Practice these phone numbers and email addresses.
Then listen and check your answers.

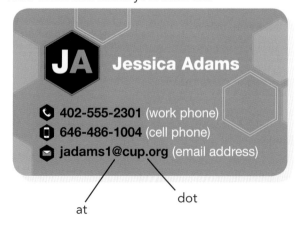

"Her name is Jessica Adams. Her work phone number is four-oh-two,
five-five-five, two-three-oh-one. Her cell . . ."

12 LISTENING Contact information

A Isabella and Joshua are making a list of classmates' phone numbers and email addresses. Listen and complete the list.

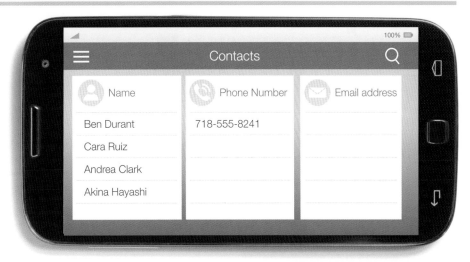

Name	Phone Number	Email address
Ben Durant	718-555-8241	
Cara Ruiz		
Andrea Clark		
Akina Hayashi		

B CLASS ACTIVITY Make a list of your classmates' names, phone numbers, and email addresses.

A: What's your name?
B: I'm Maria Ventura.

A: And what's your phone number?
B: It's 323-555-7392.

13 INTERCHANGE 1 Celebrity classmates

Meet some "famous classmates." Go to Interchange 1 on page 114.

14 SPEAKING Saying good-bye

A Listen and practice.

Bye, Robin.

See you tomorrow, Preeti.

See you later, Mike.

Bye-bye, Mike.

Good night, Jake.

Good-bye, Liz. Have a good evening!

Good-bye, Mr. Davis. Have a great weekend.

Thank you, Mr. Flores. You, too.

B CLASS ACTIVITY Go around the room. Say good-bye to your classmates and teacher.

2 Where are my keys?

▸ Identify and discuss personal and classroom objects
▸ Discuss the location of items

1 SNAPSHOT

▶ Listen and practice.

WHAT'S IN YOUR BAG?

☐ a laptop

☐ a cell phone

☐ an umbrella

☐ keys

☐ sunglasses

☐ an energy bar

☐ a wallet

☐ a hairbrush

Check (✓) the things in your bag.
What is one other thing in your bag?

2 ARTICLES Classroom objects

▶ **A** Listen. Complete the sentences with *a* or *an*.

1. This is _____ book.

2. This is _____ English book.

3. This is _____ eraser.

▶ | **articles** |
| --- |
| **an** + vowel sound |
| **a** + consonant sound |

4. This is _____ notebook.

5. This is _____ pen.

6. This is _____ clock.

B PAIR WORK Find and spell these things in your classroom.

backpack	chair	eraser	pen	notebook
board	desk	pencil	wall	wastebasket
poster	door	outlet	book	window

A: This is a chair.
B: How do you spell *chair*?
A: C-H-A-I-R.

3 CONVERSATION What are these?

▶ Listen and practice.

Brandon	Excuse me. What are these?
Christina	They're flash drives.
Brandon	Oh, they're cool. And what's this?
Christina	It's a tablet.
Brandon	A tablet? Really? Wow! It's great!
Christina	Yes, it is. It's a new model.
Brandon	Huh . . . and what's this?
Christina	It's a tablet case.
Brandon	Oh. It's . . . interesting . . . and different.

4 PRONUNCIATION Plural –s endings

▶ **A** Listen and practice. Notice the pronunciation of the plural **–s** endings.

s = /z/		**s** = /s/		**(e)s** = /ɪz/	
flash drive	flash drive**s**	desk	desk**s**	tablet case	tablet case**s**
cell phone	cell phone**s**	laptop	laptop**s**	class	class**es**
pencil	pencil**s**	backpack	backpack**s**	hairbrush	hairbrush**es**

B Say the plural form of these nouns. Then complete the chart.

| **phone case** | **student ID** | **paper clip** | **newspaper** | **purse** |

| **tablet** | **television** | **ticket** | **box** |

/z/	/s/	/ɪz/
		phone cases

▶ **C** Listen and check your answers.

GRAMMAR FOCUS

This/these, it/they; plurals

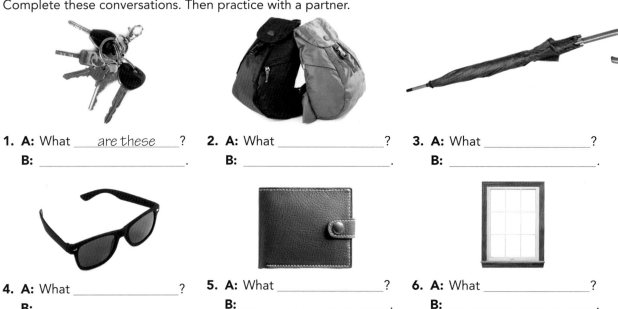

This is a laptop.

These are laptops.

What**'s this**?
It's a flash drive.

What **are these**?
They're flash drive**s**.

It**'s** = It is
They**'re** = They are

GRAMMAR PLUS *see page 133*

Complete these conversations. Then practice with a partner.

1. **A:** What ____are these____?
   B: _____.

2. **A:** What _____?
   B: _____.

3. **A:** What _____?
   B: _____.

4. **A:** What _____?
   B: _____.

5. **A:** What _____?
   B: _____.

6. **A:** What _____?
   B: _____.

6 SPEAKING What's this called?

A Listen and practice.

A: What's this called in English?
B: I don't know.
C: It's a credit card.
A: How do you spell that?
C: C-R-E-D-I-T C-A-R-D.

A: What are these called in English?
B: I think they're called headphones.
A: How do you spell that?
B: H-E-A-D-P-H-O-N-E-S.

B GROUP WORK Choose four things. Put them on a desk.
Then ask about the name and spelling of each thing.

7 CONVERSATION Where are my car keys?

▶ Listen and practice.

Lauren: Oh, no! Where are my car keys?

Matt: I don't know. Are they in your purse?

Lauren: No, they're not.

Matt: Maybe they're on the table in the restaurant.

Server: Excuse me. Are these your keys?

Lauren: Yes, they are. Thank you!

Server: You're welcome. And is this your wallet?

Lauren: Hmm. No, it's not. Where's your wallet, Matthew?

Matt: It's in my pocket. . . . Wait a minute! That *is* my wallet!

8 GRAMMAR FOCUS

▶ **Yes/No and *where* questions with *be***

Is this your wallet?
   Yes, **it is**. / No, **it's not**.
Are these your keys?
   Yes, **they are**. / No, **they're not**.

Where's your wallet?
   It's in my pocket.
Where are my keys?
   They're on the table.

GRAMMAR PLUS *see page 133*

A Complete these conversations. Then practice with a partner.

1. A: _____Is_____ this your cell phone?
   B: No, _____ not.
   A: _____ these your car keys?
   B: Yes, _____ are. Thanks!

2. A: Where _____ my glasses?
   B: Are _____ your glasses?
   A: No, they're _____.
   B: Look! _____ they in your pocket?
   A: Yes, _____. Thanks!

3. A: Where _____ your headphones?
   B: _____ on the table.
   A: No, _____ not. They're *my* headphones!
   B: You're right. My headphones _____ in my backpack.

4. A: _____ this my umbrella?
   B: No, _____ not. It's my umbrella.
   A: Sorry. _____ is my umbrella?
   B: _____ on your chair.
   A: Oh, you're right!

B GROUP WORK Choose one of your things and put it in a bag. Then choose something from the bag that is not your object. Find the owner of this object.

A: Is this your pen, Akiko?
B: No, it's not.
C: Are these your keys, Marcos?
D: Let me see. Yes, they are.

9 WORD POWER Prepositions; article *the*

A Listen and practice.

Where is **the** cell phone?
The cell phone is in **the** box.

in

in front of

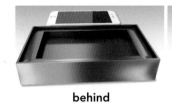

behind

on

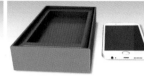

next to

under

B Complete these sentences. Then listen and check your answers.

DAILY TIMES

WORLD LEADERS MEETING TODAY!

VOTE!

ECONOMIC GROWTH

1. The books are *in the backpack* .

2. The flash drives are _____ _____.

3. The newspaper is _____ _____.

4. The chair is _____ _____.

5. The wallet is _____ _____.

6. The glasses are _____ _____.

C PAIR WORK Ask and answer questions about the pictures in part B.

A: Where are the books?

B: They're in the backpack.

10 LISTENING Emily's things

Listen. Where are Emily's things? Check (✓) the correct locations.

1. sunglasses	☐ on the table	☐ in her purse
2. ID	☐ in her wallet	☐ in front of the clock
3. headphones	☐ on the chair	☐ next to the television
4. tablet	☐ on the table	☐ under the table

11 SPEAKING Where are Kevin's things?

PAIR WORK Help Kevin find his things. Ask and answer questions.

| cell phone | hairbrush | laptop | umbrella | glasses | keys | tablet | credit card |

A: Where's his cell phone?
B: It's under the chair.

12 INTERCHANGE 2 Find the differences

Compare two pictures of a room. Go to Interchange 2 on page 115.

Units 1–2 Progress check

SELF-ASSESSMENT

How well can you do these things? Check (✓) the boxes.

I can . . .	Very well	OK	A little
Introduce myself and other people (Ex. 1)	☐	☐	☐
Say hello and good-bye (Ex. 1)	☐	☐	☐
Exchange contact information (Ex. 2)	☐	☐	☐
Understand names for everyday objects and possessions (Ex. 3)	☐	☐	☐
Ask and answer questions about where things are (Ex. 4, 5)	☐	☐	☐

1 SPEAKING How are you?

A Complete the conversation. Use the sentences and questions in the box.

Francisco	_Hi. How are you?_
Nicole	I'm fine, thanks. _____
Francisco	Pretty good, thanks. _____
Nicole	And I'm Nicole White.
Francisco	_____
Nicole	Nice to meet you, too. _____
Francisco	Yes, I am.
Nicole	_____
Francisco	See you in class.

> My name is Francisco Diaz.
> Oh, are you in my English class?
> How about you?
> ✓ Hi. How are you?
> It's nice to meet you, Nicole.
> Well, have a good day.

B PAIR WORK Practice the conversation from part A. Use your own information.
Then introduce your partner to a classmate.

"Monica, this is my friend. His name is Kenta. . . ."

2 SPEAKING Is your phone number . . . ?

CLASS ACTIVITY Write your phone number on
a piece of paper. Then put the papers in a bag.
Take a different paper and find the owner.
Write his or her name on the paper.

A: Kamal, is your phone number 781-555-1532?
B: No, it's not. Sorry!
A: Bruna, is your . . . ?

3 LISTENING What's this? What are these?

▶ Listen to the conversations. Number the pictures from 1 to 6.

☐   ☐   ☐   ☐   ☐   ☐

4 SPEAKING What's wrong with this room?

A What's wrong with this room? Make a list. Find 10 things.

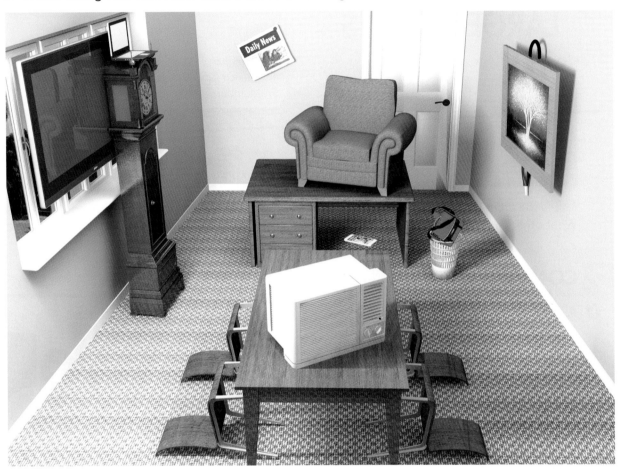

B PAIR WORK Ask and answer *Where* questions about the picture.

A: Where's the chair?
B: It's on the desk.

5 SPEAKING Yes or No game

Write five yes/no questions about the picture in Exercise 4. Make three questions with "yes" answers and two questions with "no" answers. Then ask a partner the questions.

A: Is the chair behind the clock?   **A:** Is the clock in front of the television?
B: No, it isn't.   **B:** Yes, it is.

3 Where are you from?

▸ Discuss cities, countries, nationalities, and languages
▸ Discuss people's appearances, personalities, and ages

1 SNAPSHOT

▶ Listen and practice.

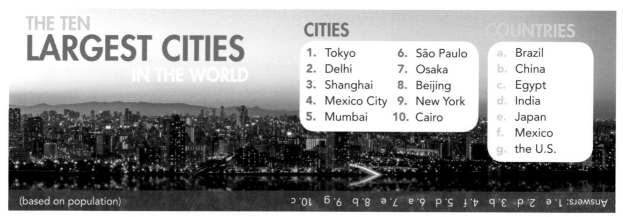

THE TEN LARGEST CITIES IN THE WORLD

(based on population)

CITIES

1. Tokyo		6. São Paulo
2. Delhi		7. Osaka
3. Shanghai		8. Beijing
4. Mexico City		9. New York
5. Mumbai		10. Cairo

COUNTRIES

a. Brazil
b. China
c. Egypt
d. India
e. Japan
f. Mexico
g. the U.S.

Answers: 1. e   2. d   3. b   4. f   5. d   6. a   7. e   8. b   9. g   10. c

Match the cities with the countries. Then check your answers at the bottom of the Snapshot.
What other large cities are in each country? What large cities are in your country?

2 CONVERSATION Are you from Rio?

▶ **A** Listen and practice.

Alexis Are you from Florida, Felipe?

Felipe Well, my family is in Florida now, but we're from Brazil originally.

Alexis Really? My father is Brazilian – from Rio de Janeiro!

Felipe So, is your first language Portuguese?

Alexis No, it's English. Are you from Rio?

Felipe No, we're not. We're from São Paulo.

▶ **B** Listen to Alexis and Felipe talk to Fernando, Nanami, and Sophia. Check (✓) True or False.

	True	False
1. Fernando is from Spain.	☐	☐
2. Nanami is from Japan.	☐	☐
3. Sophia's first language is French.	☐	☐

16

3 GRAMMAR FOCUS

GRAMMAR PLUS see page 134

Negative statements and yes/no questions with *be*

I'm not from Rio.	**Are you** from São Paulo?		I am.		**I'm not.**
You're not late.	**Am I** early?		you are.		**you're not.**
She's not from Japan.	**Is she** from the U.S.?		she is.		**she's not.**
He's not from Chile.	**Is he** from Mexico?	Yes,	he is.	No,	**he's not.**
It's not English.	**Is it** French?		it is.		**it's not.**
We're not from China.	**Are you** from South Korea?		we are.		**we're not.**
You're not early.	**Are we** late?		you are.		**you're not.**
They're not in India.	**Are they** in Egypt?		they are.		**they're not.**

We**'re** = we are

For a list of countries, nationalities, and languages, see the appendix at the back of the book.

A Complete the conversations. Then practice with a partner.

1. **A:** _____Are_____ Diana and Mario from Ecuador?
   B: No, _____ not. _____ from Mexico.
   A: _____ you from Mexico, too?
   B: No, _____ not . I'm from Colombia.
   A: So, _____ your first language Spanish?
   B: Yes, it _____.

2. **A:** _____ Meera from England?
   B: No, _____ not. She's from Australia.
   A: _____ she from Sydney?
   B: Yes, she _____. But her parents are from India.
   _____ not from Australia originally.
   A: _____ Meera's first language Hindi?
   B: No, _____ not. _____ English.

3. **A:** Ji-hye, _____ you and Kwang-ho from South Korea?
   B: Yes, we _____.
   A: And _____ from Seoul?
   B: No, _____ not. _____ from Busan.

Bogotá, Colombia

Busan, South Korea

B Match the questions with the answers. Then practice with a partner.

1. Are Liam and Grace from England? _d_
2. Is your first language Mandarin? _____
3. Are you Egyptian? _____
4. Is Mr. Lau from Beijing? _____
5. Is your mother from the U.K.? _____

a. No, he's not. He's from Shanghai.
b. Yes, she is. She's from London.
c. No, it's not. It's Cantonese.
d. No, they're not. They're from New Zealand.
e. Yes, we are. We're from Cairo.

C **PAIR WORK** Write five questions about your classmates.
Then ask and answer your questions with a partner.

4 PRONUNCIATION Syllable stress

A Listen and practice. Notice the syllable stress.

● •	• ●	● • •	• ● •
China	Brazil	Canada	Malaysia
Turkey	Japan	Mexico	Morocco
______	______	______	______
______	______	______	______

B What is the syllable stress in these words? Add the words to the chart in part A. Then listen and check.

English	Spanish	Arabic	Korean
Mexican	Honduras	Chinese	Peru

C GROUP WORK Are the words in part A countries, nationalities, or languages? Make a chart and add more words.

Countries	Nationalities	Languages
Brazil	Brazilian	Portuguese
Mexico	Mexican	Spanish

5 SPEAKING Is Bruno Mars from Italy?

A Where are these people from? Check (✓) your guesses.

Bruno Mars
- ☐ Italy
- ☐ the Philippines
- ☐ the U.S.

Morena Baccarin
- ☐ Argentina
- ☐ Brazil
- ☐ the U.S.

Gael García Bernal
- ☐ Brazil
- ☐ Mexico
- ☐ Spain

Mao Asada
- ☐ China
- ☐ Japan
- ☐ South Korea

Chris Hemsworth
- ☐ Australia
- ☐ Canada
- ☐ England

B PAIR WORK Compare your guesses. Then check your answers at the bottom of the page.

A: Is Bruno Mars from Italy?
B: No, he's not.
A: Is he from the Philippines?

Answers: 1. the U.S. 2. Brazil 3. Mexico 4. Japan 5. Australia

6 CONVERSATION Who's that?

▶ **A** Listen and practice.

 Nadia Who's that?

 Ben She's my sister.

 Nadia She's really pretty. What's her name?

 Ben Madison. We call her Maddie.

 Nadia Madison . . . that's a beautiful name. How old is she?

 Ben She's twenty-eight.

 Nadia And what's she like? Is she nice?

 Ben Well, she's shy, but she's really kind.

 Nadia And who's that little girl?

 Ben That's her daughter Mia. She's six years old.

 Nadia She's cute!

 Ben Yes, she is – and she's very smart, too.

7 SPEAKING Numbers and ages

▶ **A** Listen and practice.

11 eleven	**21** twenty-one	**40** forty
12 twelve	**22** twenty-two	**50** fifty
13 thirteen	**23** twenty-three	**60** sixty
14 fourteen	**24** twenty-four	**70** seventy
15 fifteen	**25** twenty-five	**80** eighty
16 sixteen	**26** twenty-six	**90** ninety
17 seventeen	**27** twenty-seven	**100** one hundred
18 eighteen	**28** twenty-eight	**101** one hundred (and) one
19 nineteen	**29** twenty-nine	**102** one hundred (and) two
20 twenty	**30** thirty	**103** one hundred (and) three

▶ **B** Listen and practice. Notice the word stress.

• •   • ••   • •   • ••   • •   • ••   • •   • ••

thirteen – thirty   fourteen – forty   fifteen – fifty   sixteen – sixty

C PAIR WORK Look at the people in Ben's family for one minute. How old are they? Close your books and tell your partner.

A. Carol – 76   **B.** Richard – 50   **C.** Karen – 49   **D.** Amber – 17   **E.** Jay and Joe – 10

▶ Wh-questions with *be*

What's your name?
My name is Sophia.

Where are you from?
I'm from Canada.

How are you today?
I'm fine, thanks.

Who's that?
She's my sister.

How old is she?
She's twenty-eight.

What's she like?
She's very nice.

Who are they?
They're my classmates.

Where are they from?
They're from San Francisco.

What's San Francisco like?
It's very beautiful.

Who**'s** = Who **is**

GRAMMAR PLUS *see page 134*

A Complete the conversations with Wh-questions. Then practice with a partner.

1. A: Look! _Who's that_ ?
　B: Oh, she's a new student.
　A: _____ ?
　B: I think her name is Yoo-jin.
　A: Yoo-jin? _____ ?
　B: She's from South Korea.

2. A: Hi, Brittany. _____ ?
　B: I'm fine, thanks. My friend Leandro is here this week – from Argentina.
　A: Oh, cool. _____ ?
　B: He's really friendly.
　A: _____ ?
　B: He's twenty-five years old.

3. A: Azra, _____ ?
　B: I'm from Turkey. From Ankara.
　A: _____ ?
　B: Well, Ankara is the capital of Turkey. It's very old.
　A: _____ ?
　B: My last name is Ganim.

4. A: Good morning, Luke.
　　_____ ?
　B: I'm great, thanks.
　A: Cool. _____ ?
　B: They're my friends from school.
　A: _____ ?
　B: They're from Miami, like me.

B **PAIR WORK** Write six Wh-questions about your partner and six Wh-questions about your partner's best friend. Then ask and answer the questions.

Your partner	Your partner's best friend
Where are you from?	Who's your best friend?

9 WORD POWER Describing people

▶ **A** Listen and practice.

a. pretty	**d.** talkative	**g.** funny	**j.** shy	**m.** heavy
b. handsome	**e.** friendly	**h.** quiet	**k.** short	**n.** thin
c. good-looking	**f.** kind	**i.** serious	**l.** tall	

B **PAIR WORK** Complete the chart with words from part A. Add two more words
to each list. Then describe your personality and appearance to a partner.

Personality			Appearance		
talkative			pretty		

"I'm tall, friendly, and very talkative."

10 LISTENING Wow! Who's that?

▶ Listen to three descriptions. Check (✓) the two correct words for each description.

1. Nora is . . .	2. Taylor is . . .	3. Austin is . . .
☐ tall	☐ funny	☐ short
☐ pretty	☐ pretty	☐ serious
☐ quiet	☐ handsome	☐ talkative
☐ talkative	☐ serious	☐ tall

11 INTERCHANGE 3 Let's talk!

Talk to your classmates. Go to Interchange 3 on page 118.

4 Is this coat yours?

▸ Discuss work and free-time clothes; colors
▸ Discuss the weather and what people are wearing

1 WORD POWER Clothes

▶ **A** Listen and practice.

Clothes for work

jacket
shirt
blouse
tie
suit
belt
pants
skirt
shoes
raincoat
dress
high heels
coat

Clothes for free time

hat
scarf
T-shirt
gloves
sweater
shorts
jeans
boots
socks
sneakers
pajamas
cap
swimsuits

B Complete the chart with words from part A.

Clothes for warm weather	Clothes for cold weather
86°F | 30°C _____	32°F | 0°C _____

C PAIR WORK Look around the classroom. What clothes do you see? Tell a partner.

"I see jeans, a sweater, boots, and . . ."

2 SPEAKING Colors

▶ **A** Listen and practice.

white	light gray	gray
dark gray	beige	light brown
brown	dark brown	black

B GROUP WORK Ask about favorite colors.

    A: What are your favorite colors?

    B: My favorite colors are orange and dark blue.

C GROUP WORK Describe the clothes in Exercise 1.

    A: The suit is black.

    B: The socks are dark blue.

3 PRONUNCIATION The letters *s* and *sh*

▶ **A** Listen and practice. Notice the pronunciation of **s** and **sh**.

    suit   **s**ocks   **s**wimsuit

    shirt   **sh**orts   **sh**oes

B Read the sentences. Pay attention to the pronunciation of **s** and **sh**.

    1. This is Jo**sh**ua's new **s**uit.

    2. These are **S**arah's purple **sh**oes!

    3. Where are my **sh**oes and **s**ocks?

    4. My **sh**orts and T-**sh**irts are blue!

4 CONVERSATION Whose jeans are these?

▶ Listen and practice.

Ashley Great! Our clothes are dry.

Jessica Hey, where is my new blouse?

Ashley What color is your blouse? Is this yours?

Jessica No, this blouse is blue. Mine is white. Wait! It *is* mine. My white blouse is . . . blue!

Ashley Oh, no! Look. It's a disaster! *All* our clothes are blue . . .

Jessica Here's the problem. It's these blue jeans. Whose jeans are these? Are they yours?

Ashley Uh, yes, they're mine. Sorry.

5 GRAMMAR FOCUS

▶ Possessives

Adjectives		Pronouns	Names	
my		**mine.**	**Jack's** tie.	s = /s/
your		**yours.**	**Taylor's** shoes.	s = /z/
These are **his** shoes.	These shoes are	**his.**	**Alex's** coat.	s = /ɪz/
her		**hers.**		
our		**ours.**	**Whose** tie is this? It's **Greg's.**	
their		**theirs.**	**Whose** shoes are these? They're **Taylor's.**	

GRAMMAR PLUS *see page 135*

A Complete the conversations with the correct words in parentheses. Then practice with a partner.

1. A: This isn't _____my_____ (my / mine) raincoat. Is it _____ (your / yours)?

   B: No, it's not _____ (my / mine). Ask Emma. Maybe it's _____ (her / hers).

2. A: Hey! These aren't _____ (our / ours) sneakers!

   B: You're right. _____ (Our / Ours) are over there.

3. A: Are these _____ (your / yours) gloves, Erin?

   B: No, they're not _____ (my / mine). Maybe they are Logan's. _____ (His / Your) gloves are gray.

4. A: _____ (Whose / Yours) T-shirts are these? Are they Hayley's and Brad's?

   B: No, they're not _____ (their / theirs) T-shirts. _____ (Their / Theirs) are white, not blue.

B CLASS ACTIVITY Put one of your things in a box. Then choose a different thing from the box. Go around the class and find the owner.

A: Laura, are these sunglasses yours?
B: No, they're not mine. Maybe they're Joon-ho's.

C: Wei, is this your pen?
D: Yes, it is.

6 LISTENING Her sneakers are purple.

▶ **A** Listen to someone describe six people. Number the pictures from 1 to 6 in the order you hear them.

☐ Alicia   1 Sarah   ☐ Andrea   ☐ Amanda   ☐ Cody   ☐ Kyle

B PAIR WORK Now talk about the people. What colors are their clothes?

A: What color is Alicia's jacket?
B: It's beige.

7 SNAPSHOT

▶ Listen and practice.

WEATHER AND SEASONS AROUND THE WORLD

It's spring in São Paulo, Brazil.
It's warm. It's very sunny.

It's summer in Seoul, South Korea.
It's raining. It's hot and humid.

It's fall in Chicago in the U.S.
It's cool. It's cloudy and windy.

It's winter in Toronto, Canada.
It's snowing. It's very cold.

What season is it now in your town or city? What's the weather like today?
What's your favorite season?

8 CONVERSATION   Are you wearing your gloves?

▶ Listen and practice.

Ashley   Oh, no!

Jessica   What's the matter?

Ashley   It's snowing! Wow, it's so cold and windy!

Jessica   Are you wearing your gloves?

Ashley   No, I'm not. They're at home.

Jessica   What about your scarf?

Ashley   It's at home, too.

Jessica   Well, you're wearing your coat.

Ashley   But my coat isn't very warm. And I'm not wearing boots!

Jessica   OK. Let's take a taxi.

Ashley   Good idea!

▶ **Present continuous statements; conjunctions**

		OR:	Conjunctions
I **'m**	I **'m not**		It's snowing, **and** it's windy.
You **'re**	You **'re not**	You **aren't**	It's sunny, **but** it's cold.
She **'s wearing shoes.**	She **'s not**	She **isn't wearing boots.**	It's windy, **so** it's very cold.
We **'re**	We **'re not**	We **aren't**	
They **'re**	They **'re not**	They **aren't**	
It **'s snowing.**	It **'s not**	It **isn't raining.**	

GRAMMAR PLUS *see page 135*

A Complete these sentences from a travel show on TV. Then compare with a partner.

My name is Dylan Jones. I _'m wearing_____
a new gray suit. I _____
new black shoes, too. It's raining, but I _____
_____ a raincoat.

It's very hot and sunny today. Michael
_____ light blue shorts and white
sneakers. He _____ a white
T-shirt, but he _____ a cap.

Adriana Fuentes is from Mexico. She
_____ a pretty yellow dress
and a brown belt. She _____
high heels and a light brown jacket, but she
_____ a coat. Wow, it's
really windy!

Hee-sun and Kun-woo are here with me today.
They're 10 years old. It's really cold, so they
_____ winter clothes. They
_____ boots, gloves, hats,
and scarves. And they _____
heavy coats!

Are you **wearing** gloves?	Yes, I **am**.	No, I**'m not**.
Is she **wearing** boots?	Yes, she **is**.	No, she**'s not**./No, she **isn't**.
Are they **wearing** sunglasses?	Yes, they **are**.	No, they**'re not**./No, they **aren't**.

GRAMMAR PLUS *see page 135*

B PAIR WORK Ask and answer these questions about the people in part A.

1. Is Dylan wearing a gray suit?
2. Is he wearing a raincoat?
3. Is he wearing black shoes?
4. Is Michael wearing jeans?
5. Is he wearing a T-shirt?
6. Is he wearing a cap?

7. Is Adriana wearing a skirt?
8. Is she wearing a jacket?
9. Is she wearing high heels?
10. Are Hee-sun and Kun-woo wearing swimsuits?
11. Are they wearing gloves and hats?
12. Are they wearing sneakers?

A: Is Dylan wearing a gray suit?
B: Yes, he is. Is he wearing a raincoat?
A: No, he's not. OR No, he isn't.

adjective + noun

My suit is **black**.
I'm wearing **a black suit**.

C Write four more questions about the people in part A.
Then ask a partner the questions.

10 LISTENING You look great in pink.

▶ **A** Listen. What are their names? Write the
names **Brittany**, **Ryan**, **John**, **Robert**,
Kayla, and **Amber** in the correct boxes.

B GROUP WORK Ask questions about
the people in the picture.

A: Is John wearing a brown jacket?
B: Yes, he is.
C: Is he wearing a cap?

C GROUP WORK Write five questions about
your classmates. Then ask and answer the
questions.

Are Maria and Bruno wearing jeans?
Is Bruno wearing a red shirt?

Kayla

11 INTERCHANGE 4 Celebrity fashions

What are your favorite celebrities wearing? Go to Interchange 4 on pages 116–117.

Units 3–4 Progress check

SELF-ASSESSMENT

How well can you do these things? Check (✓) the boxes.

I can . . .	Very well	OK	A little
Ask and answer questions about countries of origin, nationalities, and languages (Ex. 1)	☐	☐	☐
Understand descriptions of people (Ex. 2)	☐	☐	☐
Ask and answer questions about people's appearance and personality (Ex. 2, 5)	☐	☐	☐
Ask and answer questions about people's possessions (Ex. 3)	☐	☐	☐
Talk and write about my and other people's favorite things (Ex. 4)	☐	☐	☐
Ask and answer questions about what people are wearing (Ex. 5)	☐	☐	☐

1 SPEAKING Interview with my classmates

Match the questions with the answers. Then ask and answer the questions with a partner. Answer with your own information.

1. Are you from Argentina? __h__
2. Where are you and your family from? _____
3. What is your hometown like? _____
4. Is English your first language? _____
5. Who is your best friend? _____
6. How old is your best friend? _____
7. Is our teacher from the U.S.? _____
8. Are our classmates friendly? _____

a. It's very beautiful.
b. Yes, she is.
c. We're from Montevideo.
d. My best friend is Takuya.
e. Yes, they are.
f. No, it's not. It's Spanish.
g. He's nineteen.
h. No, I'm not. I'm from Uruguay.

2 LISTENING Where's your friend Jacob?

▶ **A** Listen to four conversations. Check (✓) the correct description for each person. You will check more than one adjective.

1. Jacob
- ☐ tall
- ☐ short
- ☐ funny
- ☐ serious
- ☐ nice
- ☐ shy

2. Monica
- ☐ tall
- ☐ talkative
- ☐ pretty
- ☐ shy
- ☐ nice
- ☐ friendly

3. Hannah
- ☐ thin
- ☐ short
- ☐ quiet
- ☐ shy
- ☐ serious
- ☐ funny

4. Ki-nam
- ☐ tall
- ☐ short
- ☐ funny
- ☐ friendly
- ☐ talkative
- ☐ quiet

B Write five yes/no questions about the people in part A. Then ask a partner the questions.

Is Jacob tall?

Is Monica thin?

3 SPEAKING Are these your clothes?

CLASS ACTIVITY Draw three pictures of clothes on different pieces of paper. Then put the papers in a bag. Take three different papers, go around the class, and find the owners.

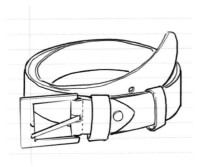  

A: Anna, is this your belt?
B: No, it's not mine. Maybe it's Miki's.

A: Ji-hun, are these your sneakers?
C: Yes, they're mine. Thanks!

4 SPEAKING Similar or different?

A Write your favorite things in the chart. Then ask a partner about his or her favorite things. Write them in the chart.

Favorite	Me	My partner
1. season		
2. color		
3. clothes		

B Compare answers. What's the same? What's different? Write sentences.

Spring is my favorite season, and it's Mariana's favorite season. That's the same.

My favorite color is green, but Mariana's favorite color is red, so that's different.

5 SPEAKING I'm thinking of . . .

GROUP WORK Think of a student in the class. Your classmates ask yes/no questions to guess the student.

A: I'm thinking of a student in this class.
B: Is it a woman?
A: Yes, it is.
C: Is she short?
A: No, she isn't.
D: Is she wearing blue jeans?

WHAT'S NEXT?

Look at your Self-assessment again. Do you need to review anything?

What time is it?

▸ Discuss cities and time zones
▸ Discuss people's activities

1 SNAPSHOT

▶ Listen and practice.

Time Zones

Mexico City 10:00 A.M.   New York 11:00 A.M.   Dubai 7:00 P.M.   Seoul 12:00 A.M.

Is your city or town in the same time zone as one of these cities?
What other events or shows are on television in different time zones?

2 CONVERSATION It's two o'clock in the morning!

▶ A Listen and practice.

2:00 A.M. ▾

Amar Hello?

Brian Hi, Amar! This is Brian. I'm calling from New York.

Amar Brian? Wait. . . . Where are you?

Brian I'm home on vacation, remember? I'm calling about the soccer game. Great game!

Amar Oh, that's good. But what time is it there?

Brian It's 2:00 P.M. And it's two o'clock in Australia, too. Right?

Amar That's right – it's two o'clock in the morning!

Brian 2:00 A.M.? Oh, of course! I'm really sorry.

Amar That's OK. Congratulations on the game!

2:00 P.M. ▴

3 GRAMMAR FOCUS

▶ What time is it?

 It's two **o'clock**.

 It's two-oh-five.
It's five **after** two.

 It's two-fifteen.
It's **a quarter after** two.

 It's two-thirty.

 It's two-forty.
It's twenty **to** three.

 It's two forty-five.
It's **a quarter to** three.

GRAMMAR PLUS see page 136

A PAIR WORK Look at these clocks. What time is it?

1   **2**   **3**   **4**   **5**   **6**

A: What time is it?
B: It's ten after ten. OR It's ten-ten.

▶ Is it A.M. or P.M.?

It's six (o'clock) **in the morning**.
It's 6:00 A.M.

It's twelve (o'clock).
It's 12:00 P.M.
It's **noon**.

It's four (o'clock) **in the afternoon**.
It's 4:00 P.M.

It's six (o'clock) **in the evening**.
It's 6:00 P.M.

It's nine (o'clock) **at night**.
It's 9:00 P.M.

It's twelve (o'clock) **at night**.
It's 12:00 A.M.
It's midnight.

GRAMMAR PLUS see page 136

B PAIR WORK Say each time a different way.

1. It's eight o'clock in the morning. *"It's 8:00 A.M."*
2. It's three o'clock in the afternoon.
3. It's six o'clock in the evening.
4. It's twelve o'clock at night.

5. It's 10:00 A.M.
6. It's 4:00 P.M.
7. It's 7:00 P.M.
8. It's 12:00 P.M.

What time is it? **31**

4 LISTENING What time is it in Tokyo?

▶ **A** Lauren and John are calling friends in different parts of the world. Listen. What time is it in these cities?

City	Time
Vancouver	4:00 P.M.
Bangkok	
London	
Tokyo	
São Paulo	

▶ **B** Listen again. Check (✓) the correct answers.

1. Tanawat is . . . ☐ getting married. ☐ in São Paulo. ☐ sleeping.
2. Richard is . . . ☐ in London. ☐ in Bangkok. ☐ late.
3. Misaki is . . . ☐ in Tokyo. ☐ in Vancouver. ☐ watching TV.

5 CONVERSATION What are you doing?

▶ Listen and practice.

JAY   Hey, Kate!

KATE   What are you doing?

JAY   I'm cooking.

KATE   I know, but why are you cooking now? It's three o'clock in the morning!

JAY   I'm sorry, but I'm really hungry.

KATE   Hmm . . . What are you making?

JAY   Spaghetti.

KATE   With tomato sauce?

JAY   With tomato sauce and cheese.

KATE   I love spaghetti! Uh . . . I'm getting hungry, too.

JAY   Good. Let's eat!

6 PRONUNCIATION Rising and falling intonation

▶ **A** Listen and practice. Notice the intonation of the yes/no and Wh-questions.

Is he cooking?   What's he making?
Are they sleeping?   What are they doing?

▶ **B** Listen to the questions. Draw a rising arrow (⤴) for rising intonation and a falling arrow (⤵) for falling intonation.

1. ⤴   2. _____   3. _____   4. _____   5. _____   6. _____

Present continuous Wh-questions

San Diego   4:00 A.M.

What's Daniel **doing**?
He**'s sleeping** right now.

Guadalajara   6:00 A.M.

What's Leticia **doing**?
It's 6:00 A.M., so she**'s getting up**.

Washington, D.C.   7:00 A.M.

What are Lya and Erin **doing**?
They're having breakfast.

Brasilia   9:00 A.M.

What's Tiago **doing**?
He**'s going** to work.

Edinburgh   noon

What are Kim and Paul **doing**?
It's noon, so they**'re eating** lunch.

Cairo   3:00 P.M.

What's Amina **doing**?
She**'s working**.

Jakarta   7:00 P.M.

What's Tamara **doing**?
She**'s eating** dinner right now.

Osaka   9:00 P.M.

What's Kento **doing**?
He**'s checking** his messages.

Your city   00:00

What are you **doing**?
It's . . . I**'m** . . .

GRAMMAR PLUS *see page 136*

A PAIR WORK Ask and answer the questions about the pictures.

1. Who's having breakfast?
2. Who's eating dinner?
3. Where's Amina working?
4. Where's Kento checking his messages?
5. What's Daniel doing?
6. What's Tiago wearing?
7. Why is Leticia getting up?
8. Why are Kim and Paul having lunch?

spelling

sleep → sleep**ing**
get → ge**tting** (+ t)
have → hav**ing** (– e)

B GROUP WORK Write five more questions about the pictures. Then ask and answer your questions in groups.

WORD POWER What are they doing?

▶ **A** Listen and practice. *"They're dancing."*

dance	drive	listen to music	play basketball
read	ride a bike	run	shop
study	swim	take a walk	watch a movie

B PAIR WORK Ask and answer questions about the pictures in part A.

A: Are they running?   **A:** What are they doing?
B: No, they're not.   **B:** They're dancing.

C GROUP WORK Make two teams. Write an activity on a piece of paper.
Give the paper to the other team. Two members act out each activity.
Their team guesses. Can they guess the activity?

A: Are you running?   **C:** Are you riding bikes?
B: No, we're not.   **D:** Yes, we are!

riding bikes

9 **INTERCHANGE 5** What's wrong with this picture?

What's wrong with this picture? Go to Interchange 5 on page 119.

A Skim the conversation. Write the name of the correct person on each picture.

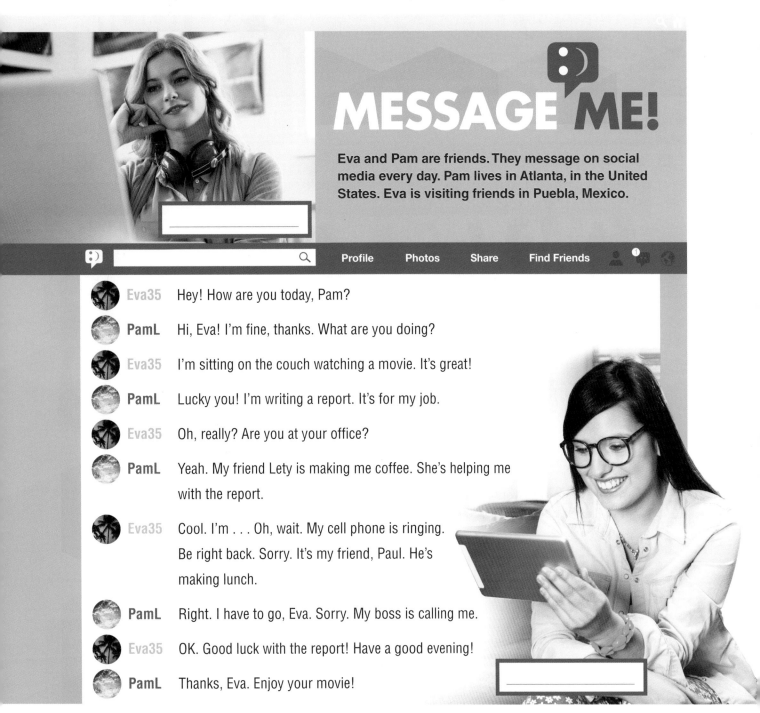

MESSAGE ME!

Eva and Pam are friends. They message on social media every day. Pam lives in Atlanta, in the United States. Eva is visiting friends in Puebla, Mexico.

Eva35	Hey! How are you today, Pam?
PamL	Hi, Eva! I'm fine, thanks. What are you doing?
Eva35	I'm sitting on the couch watching a movie. It's great!
PamL	Lucky you! I'm writing a report. It's for my job.
Eva35	Oh, really? Are you at your office?
PamL	Yeah. My friend Lety is making me coffee. She's helping me with the report.
Eva35	Cool. I'm . . . Oh, wait. My cell phone is ringing. Be right back. Sorry. It's my friend, Paul. He's making lunch.
PamL	Right. I have to go, Eva. Sorry. My boss is calling me.
Eva35	OK. Good luck with the report! Have a good evening!
PamL	Thanks, Eva. Enjoy your movie!

Profile   Photos   Share   Find Friends

B Read the conversation. Who is doing these things? Choose the correct answers.

1. Pam   Eva   . . . is watching a movie.
2. Eva   Pam   . . . is visiting friends.
3. Pam   Eva   . . . is working in an office.
4. Lety   Paul   . . . is making coffee.
5. Paul   Pam   . . . is calling Eva on her cell phone.
6. Eva   Pam's boss   . . . is calling Pam.

C PAIR WORK Think about online conversations you have with friends. What do you say? What do you ask about? Write a short conversation.

6 I ride my bike to school.

▸ Discuss transportation and family
▸ Discuss daily and weekly routines

1 SNAPSHOT

▶ Listen and practice.

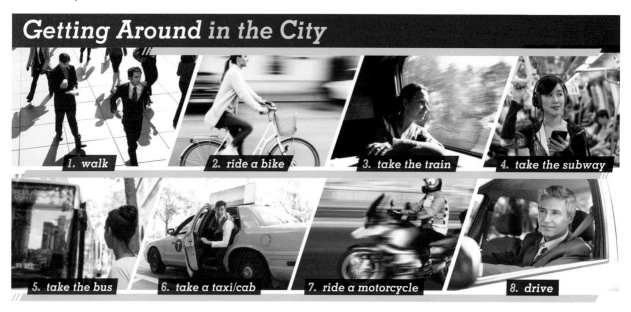

Getting Around in the City

1. walk
2. ride a bike
3. take the train
4. take the subway
5. take the bus
6. take a taxi/cab
7. ride a motorcycle
8. drive

Check (✓) the kinds of transportation you use.
What are some other kinds of transportation?

2 CONVERSATION They use public transportation.

▶ Listen and practice.

Yuto Nice car, Austin! Is it yours?

Austin No, it's my sister's. She has a new job and she drives to work.

Yuto Is her job here in the suburbs?

Austin No, it's downtown.

Yuto My parents work downtown, but they don't drive to work. They use public transportation.

Austin The bus or the train?

Yuto The bus doesn't stop near our house, so they take the train.

3 WORD POWER Family members

A PAIR WORK Complete the sentences about the Mitchell family. Then listen and check your answers.

1. Lisa is Tom's _____wife_____.
2. Megan and Austin are their _____.
3. Tom is Lisa's _____.
4. Austin is Lisa's _____.
5. Megan is Tom's _____.
6. Austin is Megan's _____.
7. Megan is Austin's _____.
8. Tom and Lisa are Austin's _____.

kids = children
mom = mother
dad = father

B PAIR WORK Who are the people in your family? What are their names?

"My father's name is Arthur. My sisters' names are Emilia and Sabrina."

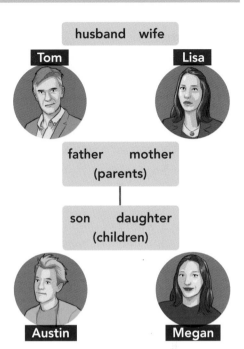

husband   wife

Tom

Lisa

father   mother
(parents)

son   daughter
(children)

Austin

Megan

brother   sister

4 GRAMMAR FOCUS

Simple present statements

I	**walk**	to school.	I	**don't live**	far from here.	**don't** = do not	
You	**ride**	your bike to school.	You	**don't live**	near here.	**doesn't** = does not	
He	**works**	near here.	He	**doesn't work**	downtown.		
She	**takes**	the bus to work.	She	**doesn't drive**	to work.		
We	**live**	with our parents.	We	**don't live**	alone.		
They	**use**	public transportation.	They	**don't need**	a car.		

GRAMMAR PLUS *see page 137*

A Tom Mitchell is talking about his family. Complete the sentences with the correct verb forms. Then compare with a partner.

1. My family and I _____live_____ (live / lives) in the suburbs. My wife and I _____ (work / works) near here, so we _____ (walk / walks) to work. Our daughter Megan _____ (work / works) downtown, so she _____ (drive / drives) to work. Our son _____ (don't / doesn't) drive. He _____ (ride / rides) his bike to school.

2. My parents _____ (live / lives) in the city. My mother _____ (take / takes) the subway to work. My father is retired, so he _____ (don't / doesn't) work now. He also _____ (use / uses) public transportation, so they _____ (don't / doesn't) need a car.

verb endings: *he, she, it*

walk → walk**s**
ride → ride**s**
study → stud**ies**
watch → watch**es**

I ride my bike to school. **37**

▶ **Simple present statements with irregular verbs**

I/you/we/they	he/she/it
I **have** a bike.	My mother **has** a car.
We **do** our homework every day.	My father **does** a lot of work at home.
My parents **go** to work by train.	The train **goes** downtown.

GRAMMAR PLUS *see page 137*

B Yuto is talking about his family and his friend Austin. Complete the sentences. Then compare with a partner.

1. My parents ____have____ (have / has) a house in the suburbs. My mom and dad _____ (go / goes) downtown to work. My parents are very busy, so I _____ (do / does) a lot of work at home.

2. My brother doesn't live with us. He _____ (have / has) an apartment in the city. He _____ (go / goes) to school all day, and he _____ (do / does) his homework at night.

3. I _____ (have / has) a new friend. His name is Austin. We _____ (go / goes) to the same school, and sometimes we _____ (do / does) our homework together.

C PAIR WORK Tell your partner about your family.

"I have one brother and two sisters. My brother is a teacher. He has a car, so he drives to work."

5 PRONUNCIATION Third-person singular –s endings

▶ Listen and practice. Notice the pronunciation of the **–s** endings.

s = /s/	**s = /z/**	**(e)s = /ɪz/**	*irregular*
take tak**es**	drive driv**es**	dance danc**es**	do do**es**
sleep sleep**s**	study studi**es**	watch watch**es**	have ha**s**

6 CONVERSATION What time do you get up?

▶ Listen and practice.

Paige: Let's go to the park Sunday morning.

Adam: Good idea, but let's go in the afternoon. I sleep late on weekends.

Paige: What time do you get up?

Adam: I get up at noon.

Paige: Really? That's late. Do you eat breakfast at noon?

Adam: Yeah. What time do *you* get up?

Paige: At ten o'clock.

Adam: Oh, that's early for a Sunday.

Paige: Hey, I have an idea! Let's eat at Park Café. They serve breakfast all day!

Simple present questions

Do you **get up** early on Sundays?
 No, I **get up** late.

Does he **eat** breakfast at seven o'clock?
 No, he **eats** breakfast at seven-thirty.

Do they **take** a taxi to class?
 No, they **take** the bus.

What time do you **get up**?
 At noon.

What time does she have dinner?
 At eight o'clock.

When do they **take** the subway?
 On Mondays and Wednesdays.

GRAMMAR PLUS *see page 137*

A Complete the questions with *do* or *does*.

1. _____Do_____ you get up late on Sundays?
2. _____ you have lunch at home every day?
3. What time _____ your father leave work on Fridays?
4. _____ your mother cook on weekdays?
5. _____ your father shop on Saturdays?
6. _____ you take a walk in the evening?
7. When _____ you listen to music?
8. What time _____ you check your email?
9. What time _____ your parents have dinner?
10. When _____ you study English?
11. _____ your best friend ride a bike on weekends?
12. _____ your father drive to work every morning?

time expressions	
early	**in** the morning
late	**in** the afternoon
every day	**in** the evening
at 9:00	**on** Sundays
at noon/midnight	**on** weekdays
at night	**on** weekends

B **PAIR WORK** Ask and answer the questions from part A.
Use time expressions from the box.

A: Do you get up late on Sundays?
B: No, I don't. I get up at eight o'clock. I play basketball on Sunday mornings.

C Unscramble the questions to complete the conversations.
Then ask a partner the questions. Answer with your
own information.

1. **A:** _What time do you eat dinner_____?
   you / what time / dinner / do / eat
   B: At 7:00 P.M.

2. **A:** _____?
   you / every morning / check your messages / do
   B: Yes, I check my messages on the bus every morning.

3. **A:** _____?
   at / start / does / seven o'clock / this class
   B: No, this class starts at eight o'clock.

4. **A:** _____?
   listen to music / you / do / when
   B: I listen to music in the evening.

5. **A:** _____?
   on weekends / you and your friends / do / play sports
   B: Yes, we play volleyball on Saturdays.

8 LISTENING Kayla's weekly routine

▶ Listen to Kayla talk about her weekly routine. Check (✓) the days she does each thing.

	Monday	Tuesday	Wednesday	Thursday	Friday	Saturday	Sunday
get up early	☐	☐	☐	☐	☐	☐	☐
go to work	☐	☐	☐	☐	☐	☐	☐
play tennis	☐	☐	☐	☐	☐	☐	☐
go shopping	☐	☐	☐	☐	☐	☐	☐
see friends	☐	☐	☐	☐	☐	☐	☐
dinner with family	☐	☐	☐	☐	☐	☐	☐
study	☐	☐	☐	☐	☐	☐	☐

9 SPEAKING My weekly routine

A What do you do every week? Write your routine in the chart.

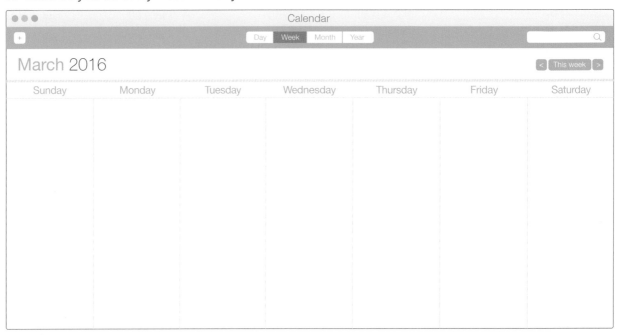

B GROUP WORK Discuss your weekly routines.
Ask and answer questions.

A: I play tennis on Sunday mornings.
B: What do you do on Sunday afternoons?
A: I see my friends. We watch movies or play games.
What about you?
C: On Sundays, I have lunch with my parents. In the
afternoon, we talk or take a walk.

10 INTERCHANGE 6 Class survey

Find out more about your classmates.
Go to Interchange 6 on page 120.

A Scan the interview. What's unusual about Mike's job?

What's your
schedule like?

Every week, we interview someone with an unusual schedule. In this week's interview, we meet Mike Watts, a professional "sleeper." Yes, that's correct. Mike's job pays him to sleep! Here, Mike talks to us about his schedule.

News Now:	Hi Mike, thanks for talking to us. What's your schedule like?
Mike:	Hi there! My schedule's strange, but I love it. I go to bed at 10:00 P.M. in a different hotel room every night.
News Now:	Wow! That's cool! Do you get up early?
Mike:	Yes, I get up at 6:00 A.M. I'm an early bird! I like the morning. At 8:00 A.M., I have a big breakfast in the hotel restaurant.
News Now:	So, who pays you to do that?
Mike:	I work for a travel blog. They pay me to stay in different hotels and write about them. People read the blog and go to the hotels. Right now, I'm at a hotel in Finland, Hotel Finn.
News Now:	And what do you do before you go to bed?
Mike:	Every afternoon, from 2:00 P.M. to 4:00 P.M., I write about each room. I talk about the bed, the lights, the noise . . .
News Now:	Who reads the blog?
Mike:	Lots of different people read it. Business people, tourists, travel agencies . . . people who want to know about hotels, really!
News Now:	What do you do in the evening?
Mike:	At 7:00 P.M., I talk to the hotel manager. Then I go to my new room and go to bed.
News Now:	Do you like sleeping?
Mike:	Yes, I do! I'm very good at it!

B Read the article. Number the activities in Mike's schedule from 1 to 5.
Then answer the questions. Write the times.

_____ **a.** Mike writes about each room.   _____ **d.** He goes to his new room.

__1__ **b.** He gets up.   _____ **e.** He has a big breakfast.

_____ **c.** He talks to the hotel manager.

1. What time does Mike write about each room? _____
2. What time does he get up? _____
3. What time does he talk to the hotel manager? _____
4. What time does he go to bed? _____
5. What time does he have breakfast? _____

C Are you an "early bird," like Mike?
Or are you a "night owl"?
Write five sentences about your
schedule. Compare with a partner.

early bird

night owl

Units 5–6 Progress check

SELF-ASSESSMENT

How well can you do these things? Check (✓) the boxes.

I can . . .	Very well	OK	A little
Understand times and descriptions of activities (Ex. 1)	☐	☐	☐
Ask and answer questions about present activities (Ex. 2)	☐	☐	☐
Talk about personal routines (Ex. 3)	☐	☐	☐
Ask and answer questions about routines (Ex. 4)	☐	☐	☐
Ask and answer questions about celebrities' appearances and activities (Ex. 5)	☐	☐	☐

1 LISTENING I'm calling from Los Angeles.

▶ It's 9:00 A.M. in Los Angeles. Stephanie is calling friends around the world.
Listen to the conversations and complete the chart.

	1. Chelsea	2. Carlos	3. Nicholas
City	New York		
Time			
Activity			

2 SPEAKING We're on vacation!

Student A: Imagine your classmates are on vacation. Student B calls you. Ask questions about your classmates.

Student B: Imagine you are on vacation with your classmates. Call Student A. Answer Student A's questions about your classmates.

A: Hello?
B: Hi, it's . . . . I'm on vacation in . . .
A: In . . . ? Wow! What are you doing?
B: . . .
A: Who are you with?
B: . . .
A: What's he/she doing?
B: . . .
A: Well, have fun. Bye!

3 SPEAKING One day in my week

A Choose one day of the week and write it in the blank.
What do you do on this day? Complete the chart.

	Day:
In the morning	
In the afternoon	
In the evening	
At night	

B PAIR WORK Tell your partner about your routine on the day from part A.

A: On Saturdays, I exercise in the morning. I run in the park with my friends.
B: What time do you run?
A: We run at 9:00.

4 SPEAKING Lifestyle survey

A Answer the questions in the chart. Check (✓) Yes or No.

	Yes	No	Name
1. Do you live with your parents?	☐	☐	
2. Do both your parents work?	☐	☐	
3. Do you play video games at night?	☐	☐	
4. Do you eat dinner with your family?	☐	☐	
5. Do you stay at home on weekends?	☐	☐	
6. Do you work on Saturdays?	☐	☐	

B CLASS ACTIVITY Go around the class and find classmates with the same answers.
Write their names in the chart. Try to write a different name on each line.

5 SPEAKING Guess who!

GROUP WORK Think of a famous person. Your classmates ask
yes/no questions to guess the person.

Is it a man? a woman?	Does he/she speak English?
Does he/she live in . . . ?	Does he/she play soccer? basketball?
Is he/she a singer? an actor?	Does he/she wear glasses?

WHAT'S NEXT?

Look at your Self-assessment again. Do you need to review anything?

7 Does it have a view?

▸ Describe houses and apartments
▸ Discuss furniture and dream homes

1 SNAPSHOT

▶ Listen and practice.

Home Sweet Home

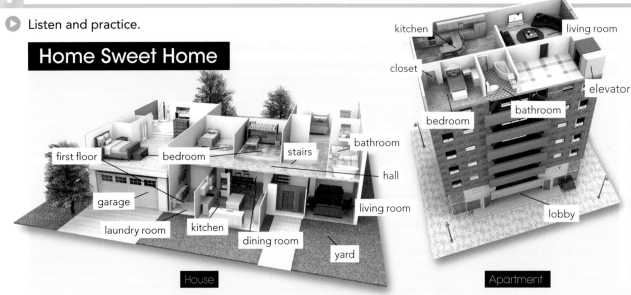

kitchen
living room
closet
elevator
bathroom
bedroom

first floor
bedroom
stairs
bathroom
hall
garage
living room
laundry room
kitchen
lobby
dining room
yard

House
Apartment

What rooms are in houses in your country? What rooms are in apartments?
What rooms are in your house or apartment? What is your favorite room?

2 CONVERSATION Do you live downtown?

▶ Listen and practice.

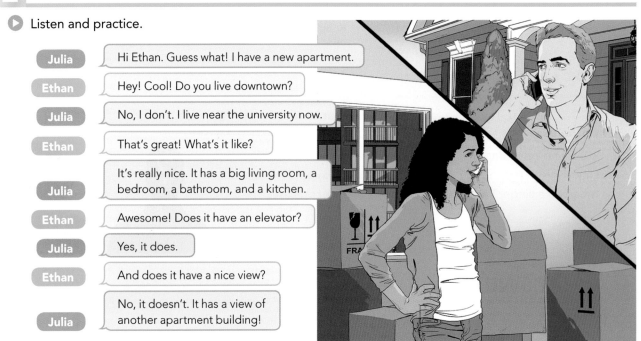

Julia Hi Ethan. Guess what! I have a new apartment.

Ethan Hey! Cool! Do you live downtown?

Julia No, I don't. I live near the university now.

Ethan That's great! What's it like?

Julia It's really nice. It has a big living room, a bedroom, a bathroom, and a kitchen.

Ethan Awesome! Does it have an elevator?

Julia Yes, it does.

Ethan And does it have a nice view?

Julia No, it doesn't. It has a view of another apartment building!

GRAMMAR FOCUS

▶ **Simple present short answers**

Do you **live** in an apartment?	**Does** Ethan **live** in a house?
Yes, I **do**. / No, I **don't**.	Yes, he **does**. / No, he **doesn't**.
Do the bedrooms **have** closets?	**Does** the house **have** a yard?
Yes, they **do**. / No, they **don't**.	Yes, it **does**. / No, it **doesn't**.

GRAMMAR PLUS *see page 138*

A Complete the conversation. Then practice with a partner.

Julia _____Do_____ you _____live_____ in an apartment?

Ethan No, I _____. I _____ in a house.

Julia _____ it _____ a yard?

Ethan Yes, it _____.

Julia That sounds nice. _____ you _____ alone?

Ethan No, I _____. I _____ with my family.

Julia _____ you _____ any brothers or sisters?

Ethan Yes, I _____. I _____ four sisters.

Julia Really? _____ your house _____ many bedrooms?

Ethan Yes, it _____. It _____ four.

Julia _____ you _____ your own bedroom?

Ethan Yes, I _____. I'm really lucky.

B PAIR WORK Read the conversation in part A again. Ask and answer these questions about Ethan.

1. Does he live in an apartment?
2. Does his house have a yard?
3. Does he live alone?
4. Does he have his own room?

C PAIR WORK Write five questions to ask your partner about his or her home. Then ask and answer the questions.

4 **LISTENING** We have a nice yard.

▶ Listen to four people describe their homes. Number the pictures from 1 to 4.

▶ **A** Listen and practice.

an armchair   a stove   curtains   pictures

a bed   a table   a coffee table

a microwave   lamps   a sofa

a desk   a refrigerator   a coffee maker   a dresser   chairs

a mirror   a bookcase   a rug   cupboards

B Which rooms have the things in part A? Complete the chart.

A kitchen has . . .	a table a stove
A dining room has . . .	a table
A living room has . . .	
A bedroom has . . .	

C GROUP WORK What furniture is in your house or apartment? Tell your classmates.

"My living room has a sofa, a bookcase, and a rug . . ."

6 CONVERSATION I really need some furniture.

▶ Listen and practice.

Eric This apartment is great, Lara.

Lara Thanks. I love it, but I really need some furniture.

Eric What do you need?

Lara Oh, lots of things. For example, there are some chairs in the kitchen, but there isn't a table.

Eric That's true. And there's no sofa in the living room.

Lara And there aren't any armchairs, there isn't a rug . . . There's only this lamp!

Eric So let's go shopping next weekend!

7 GRAMMAR FOCUS

▶ **There is, there are**

There's a bed in the bedroom.	**There are some** chairs in the kitchen.	There's = There is
There's no sofa in the bedroom.	**There are no** chairs in the living room.	
There isn't a table in the kitchen.	**There aren't any** chairs in the living room.	

GRAMMAR PLUS *see page 138*

A Look at the picture of Ann's apartment. Complete the sentences. Then practice with a partner.

1. _____There's no_____ dresser in the bedroom.
2. _____ chairs in the kitchen.
3. _____ lamp in the living room.
4. _____ refrigerator.
5. _____ rugs on the floor.
6. _____ curtains on the windows.
7. _____ armchair in the bedroom.
8. _____ books in the bookcase.

B Write five sentences about things you have or don't have in your home. Then compare with a partner.

There are two sofas in my living room.

8 INTERCHANGE 7 Find the differences

Compare two apartments. Go to Interchange 7 on page 121.

9 PRONUNCIATION Words with *th*

A Listen and practice. Notice the pronunciation of /θ/ and /ð/.

/ð/   /θ/   /ð/   /ð/   /θ/   /θ/

There are **th**irteen rooms in **th**is house. **Th**e house has **th**ree ba**th**rooms.

B **PAIR WORK** List other words with /θ/ and /ð/. Then use them to write two sentences. Read them aloud.

There are thirty-three books on their bookcase.

10 LISTENING A furniture website

Listen to Jacob and Courtney talk about furniture on a website. What does Courtney like? What doesn't she like? Choose ☺ (likes) or ☹ (doesn't like).

☺ ☹	armchairs	☺ ☹	a sofa
☺ ☹	a rug	☺ ☹	lamps
☺ ☹	a bookcase	☺ ☹	a mirror
☺ ☹	a coffee table	☺ ☹	curtains

11 SPEAKING My dream home

A Write a description of your dream home.

What is your dream home?
Where is it?
What rooms does it have?
What things are in the rooms?
Does it have a view?

My dream home is a loft in a big city. There is one large living room with a lot of windows. There are two bedrooms and . . .

a beach house

a loft in a big city

a country villa

B **PAIR WORK** Ask your partner about his or her dream home.

A: What is your dream home?
B: My dream home is a loft in a big city.
A: What rooms does it have?
B: Well, there is a big living room, a small kitchen . . .

a cabin in the mountains

A Scan the article. Which hotel has a room that looks like a dessert?

Unique Hotels

Which do you like – the world of science or the world of fiction?
In this week's vacation post, we discover a hotel made for fans of
nature and another hotel for fans of stories.

The Roxbury, New York, the United States   4 new

In the mountains near New York City, there's a very unusual
hotel. Its name is the Roxbury. It has many rooms, but every
single room is different. There's the Wizard's Emeralds room,
for example. It has a yellow "road" in the middle – just like in
The Wizard of Oz. There's a green shower in the bathroom
with big red flowers on the walls.

Bubble Hotel, Allauch, France   4 new

Just imagine sleeping in a giant, clear bubble in a
forest. That's exactly what happens here. At night,
hotel guests lie in bed and watch the stars and
moon. Each bubble has a comfortable bed and a
nice bathroom with a shower. There's also an
air-conditioner to keep the room cool in summer
and a heater to keep it warm when it's cold outside.

Each bubble room is different. Guests choose the
"Zen" bubble if they want to feel relaxed. Or they
stay in the "Love Nature" bubble for a beautiful view.
Sometimes there are rabbits and squirrels playing
outside. Is there anything missing? Well, yes, there
isn't a TV because no one needs a TV in a bubble!

Do you like sweet things?
Maryann's Coconut
Cream Pie room looks
just like a dessert –
good enough to eat! The
bed is round like a pie,
and the ceiling looks like
whipped cream.

How about space?
When you walk into George's
Spacepad, you see an enormous
red bathtub. It glows in the dark!
There isn't a shower, but there are
silver curtains, crazy lights, and
two cozy sofas. It's really out of
this world!

B Read the article. What's in each hotel? Complete the sentences.

sofas	animals	moon	round bed	✓ yellow road
stars	bathtub	TV	shower	air-conditioner

At The Roxbury

1. In the Wizard's Emeralds room, there is a _____ yellow road _____.
2. There is a _____ in Maryann's Coconut Cream Pie room.
3. In George's Spacepad, there are two _____. There is a red
   _____, but there isn't a _____.

At the Bubble Hotel

4. There is a view of the _____ and the _____.
5. There is an _____ to keep the room cool.
6. There are sometimes _____ playing outside.
7. There isn't a _____.

C GROUP WORK Talk about these questions.

1. Which hotel do you like? Why?
2. Imagine you have a hotel. What do you do to make it interesting?

8 Where do you work?

▸ Discuss jobs and workplaces using simple present Wh-questions
▸ Discuss opinions about jobs using *be* + adjective and adjective + noun

1 WORD POWER Jobs

▶ **A** Match the jobs with the pictures. Then listen and practice.

a. accountant	e. doctor	i. office manager	m. security guard
b. bellhop	f. front desk clerk	✓ j. police officer	n. server
c. cashier	g. host	k. receptionist	o. taxi driver
d. chef	h. nurse	l. salesperson	p. vendor

1.   j   2.   3.   4.   5.   6.

7.   8.   9.   10.   11.

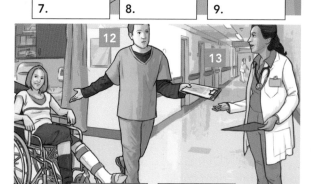

12.   13.   14.   15.   16.

B **PAIR WORK** Ask questions about the people in part A. What are their jobs?

A: What does she do?
B: She's a police officer.

2 SPEAKING Workplaces

A **PAIR WORK** Who works in these places? Complete the chart with jobs from Exercise 1. Add one more job to each list.

A: A doctor works in a hospital.   **B:** A nurse works in a hospital, too.

IN A HOSPITAL	IN AN OFFICE	IN A STORE	IN A HOTEL
a doctor			
a nurse			

B **CLASS ACTIVITY** Ask and answer *Who* questions about jobs. Use these words.

wears a uniform	sits all day	stands all day	works with a team
talks to people	works hard	works at night	makes a lot of money

A: Who wears a uniform?
B: A police officer wears a uniform.
C: A security guard wears a uniform, too.

3 CONVERSATION What does he do?

Listen and practice.

 JORDAN Where does your brother work?

 ALICIA In a hotel.

 JORDAN Oh, really? My brother works in a hotel, too. He's an accountant.

ALICIA How does he like it?

JORDAN He hates it. He doesn't like the manager.

ALICIA That's too bad. What hotel does he work for?

JORDAN The Plaza.

ALICIA That's funny. My brother works there, too.

JORDAN Oh, that's interesting. What does he do?

 ALICIA Actually, he's the manager!

▶ **Simple present Wh-questions**

Where do you **work**?	**Where does** he **work**?	**Where do** they **work**?
In a hospital.	In a hotel.	In an office.
What do you **do**?	**What does** he **do**?	**What do** they **do**?
I'm a doctor.	He's a manager.	They're accountants.
How do you **like** it?	**How does** he **like** it?	**How do** they **like** it?
I really like it.	It's OK.	They hate it.

GRAMMAR PLUS *see page 139*

A Complete these conversations. Then practice with a partner.

1. **A:** _____What_____ does your sister _____do_____?
   B: My sister? She's a teacher.
   A: _____ does she _____ it?
   B: It's difficult, but she loves it.

2. **A:** _____ does your brother _____?
   B: In an office. He's an accountant.
   A: Oh? _____ does he _____ it?
   B: He doesn't really like it.

3. **A:** _____ do your parents _____ their jobs?
   B: Oh, I guess they like them.
   A: I don't remember. _____ do they _____?
   B: In a big hospital. They're doctors.

4. **A:** _____ do you _____?
   B: I'm a student.
   A: I see. _____ do you _____ your classes?
   B: They're great. I like them a lot.

B PAIR WORK Ask questions about these people. Where do they work?
What do they do? How do they like it?

Jeff

Jodie

Chad and Tracy

A: Where does Chad work?
B: He works in . . .

5 PRONUNCIATION Reduction of *do*

▶ Listen and practice. Notice the reduction of **do**.

Where **do you** work?   Where **do they** work?

What **do you** do?   What **do they** do?

6 SNAPSHOT

▶ Listen and practice.

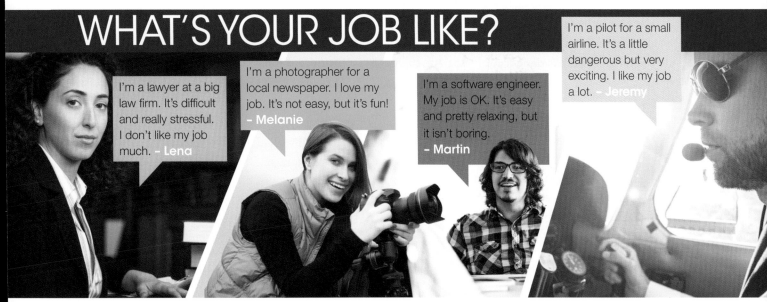

WHAT'S YOUR JOB LIKE?

I'm a lawyer at a big law firm. It's difficult and really stressful. I don't like my job much. – Lena

I'm a photographer for a local newspaper. I love my job. It's not easy, but it's fun! – Melanie

I'm a software engineer. My job is OK. It's easy and pretty relaxing, but it isn't boring. – Martin

I'm a pilot for a small airline. It's a little dangerous but very exciting. I like my job a lot. – Jeremy

Who likes his or her job? Who doesn't? Why? Why not?
What jobs do you think are interesting? What jobs are not very interesting?

7 CONVERSATION It's a dangerous job.

▶ Listen and practice.

	JACK	Hey, Paula. I hear you have a new job.
	PAULA	Yes. I'm teaching math at Lincoln High School.
	JACK	How do you like it?
	PAULA	It's difficult, but the students are terrific. How are things with you?
	JACK	Not bad. Guess what! I'm a firefighter now.
	PAULA	Really? Wow! How do you like it?
	JACK	It's a dangerous job, but it's really interesting. I love it!
	PAULA	OK, but please be careful!

8 LISTENING Is your job interesting?

▶ Listen to four people talk about their jobs. Complete the chart with the correct jobs and adjectives.

	What do they do?	What's it like?
1. Yasmin		
2. Kana		
3. Luke		
4. Brandon		

Where do you work? 53

9 GRAMMAR FOCUS

▶ **Placement of adjectives**

be + adjective	adjective + noun
A doctor's job **is stressful**.	A doctor has **a stressful job**.
A firefighter's job **is dangerous**.	A firefighter has **a dangerous job**.

GRAMMAR PLUS *see page 139*

A Write each sentence a different way. Then compare with a partner.

1. A photographer's job is interesting. <u>A photographer has an interesting job.</u>
2. A pilot's job is exciting. _____
3. A teacher's job is stressful. _____
4. A cashier has a boring job. _____
5. An accountant has a difficult job. _____
6. A receptionist has an easy job. _____

B GROUP WORK Write one job for each adjective. Do your classmates agree?

1. easy ____actor____
2. difficult _____
3. dangerous _____
4. boring _____
5. exciting _____
6. relaxing _____

A: A graphic designer has an easy job.
B: I don't agree. A graphic designer's job is difficult.
C: I think . . .

graphic designer

10 INTERCHANGE 8 The perfect job

What do you want in a job? Go to Interchange 8 on page 122.

11 SPEAKING Workday routines

GROUP WORK Ask three classmates about their jobs (or their friends'
or family members' jobs). Then tell the class.

Ask about a classmate	Ask about a classmate's friend or family member
Do you have a job?	Tell me about your . . .
Where do you work?	Where does he/she work?
What do you do, exactly?	What does he/she do, exactly?
Is your job interesting?	Is his/her job difficult?
What time do you start work?	What time does he/she start work?
When do you finish work?	When does he/she finish work?
Do you like your job?	Does he/she like his/her job?
What do you do after work?	What does he/she do after work?

12 **READING** ▶

A Do you think all jobs are boring? Think again! Look at the photos. What do these people do?

Home   Posts   Archives

Dream Jobs

Crocodile Researcher   ♡ 💬

I have a great job. I study crocodiles! It's an important job. Let me explain why. Here in Australia, we have a lot of crocodiles, but sometimes the crocodiles are sick. I want to know why. I study the food the crocodiles eat. I also learn how fast they grow and where they live. How do I do this? Well, in the morning, I take my camera, and I watch the crocodiles in the river. I take photos. Sometimes the crocodiles eat toads. Some toads make them sick and they die. I want to help the crocodiles.

Ice Cream Flavor Expert   ♡ 💬

Believe it or not, I taste ice cream for my job. Yes, it's a dream job, but it's also difficult! I work at a big ice cream company. Every day, I taste lots of different flavors three times each. Why is that? Well, I taste a little of the ice cream we make in the morning, afternoon, and at night. That way, I know that all the ice cream is good. I use my eyes first: Does the ice cream look nice? Then I taste the ice cream with a spoon: Does it taste fresh and sweet? Then I spit it out. Yes, I really spit it out!

Subscribe to our site

enter email   **Sign up**

B Read the article. Check (✓) True or False.

	True	False
1. Both people have jobs they do outside.	☐	☐
2. The crocodile researcher studies what crocodiles eat.	☐	☐
3. The crocodile researcher watches the crocodiles at night.	☐	☐
4. The ice cream flavor expert tastes each flavor three times.	☐	☐
5. Ice cream flavor experts don't look at the ice cream.	☐	☐

C What's your dream job? Why? Write a short description. Compare with a partner.

Units 7–8 Progress check

SELF-ASSESSMENT

How well can you do these things? Check (✓) the boxes.

I can . . .	Very well	OK	A little
Ask and answer questions about living spaces (Ex. 1)	☐	☐	☐
Talk about rooms and furniture (Ex. 1)	☐	☐	☐
Ask and answer questions about work (Ex. 2)	☐	☐	☐
Understand descriptions of jobs (Ex. 3)	☐	☐	☐
Give and respond to opinions about jobs (Ex. 4)	☐	☐	☐

1 SPEAKING A new apartment

A Imagine you are moving into this apartment. What things are in the rooms?
Draw pictures. Use the furniture in the box and your own ideas.

bed	chairs	desk	dresser	lamp	mirror	sofa	table

B **PAIR WORK** Ask questions about your partner's apartment.

A: I'm moving into a new apartment!
B: That's great! Where is it?
A: . . .
B: What's it like? Does it have many rooms?
A: Well, it has . . .

B: Does the . . . have . . . ?
A: . . .
B: Do you have a lot of furniture?
A: Well, there's . . . in the . . .
There are some . . . in the . . .
B: Do you have everything you need for the apartment?
A: No, I don't. There's no . . .
There isn't any . . .
There aren't any . . .
B: OK. Let's go shopping this weekend!

2 SPEAKING What does he do?

A Complete the conversations with Wh-questions.

1. A: _Where does your father work_ ?

    B: My father? He works in a store.

    A: _____?

    B: He's a salesperson.

    A: _____?

    B: He likes his job a lot!

2. A: _____?

    B: I'm an accountant.

    A: _____?

    B: I work in an office.

    A: _____?

    B: It's OK. I guess I like it.

B PAIR WORK Your partner asks the questions in part A. Answer with your own information.

3 LISTENING How do you like your job?

Listen to Rachel, Daniel, and Mai talk about their jobs. Check (✓) the correct answers.

		Where do they work?		**What do they do?**	
1.	Rachel	☐ office ☐ store		☐ receptionist ☐ doctor	
2.	Daniel	☐ hospital ☐ school		☐ nurse ☐ teacher	
3.	Mai	☐ hotel ☐ office		☐ manager ☐ front desk clerk	

4 SPEAKING Boring or interesting?

GROUP WORK What do you think of these jobs? Give your opinions.

veterinarian

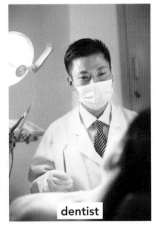
dentist

architect

hairstylist

A: I think a veterinarian has a stressful job.

B: I don't really agree. I think a veterinarian's job is relaxing.

C: Well, I think a veterinarian's job is difficult. . . .

WHAT'S NEXT?

Look at your Self-assessment again. Do you need to review anything?

Interchange activities

INTERCHANGE 1 Celebrity classmates

A Imagine you are a celebrity. Write your name, phone number, and email address on the screens.

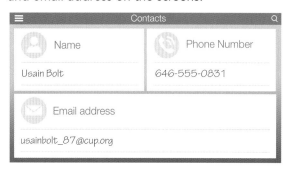

☰ Contacts 🔍

👤 Name

📞 Phone Number

Usain Bolt

646-555-0831

✉ Email address

usainbolt_87@cup.org

☰ Contacts 🔍

👤 Name

📞 Phone Number

✉ Email address

B **CLASS ACTIVITY** Go around the class. Introduce yourself to three "celebrities." Ask and answer questions to complete the screens.

A: Hi. My name is Emma Watson.

B: I'm Usain Bolt. Nice to meet you, Emma.

A: Usain, what's your email address?

B: It's U-S-A-I-N-B-O-L-T underscore eight-seven at C-U-P dot O-R-G.

A: I'm sorry. Can you repeat that?

useful expressions
I'm sorry.
Can you repeat that?
How do you spell that?

☰ Contacts 🔍

👤 Name

📞 Phone Number

✉ Email address

☰ Contacts 🔍

👤 Name

📞 Phone Number

✉ Email address

☰ Contacts 🔍

👤 Name

📞 Phone Number

✉ Email address

Emma Watson

Usain Bolt

PAIR WORK   How are the two pictures different? Ask questions to find the differences.

A: Where are the sunglasses?
B: In picture 1, they're on the bicycle.
A: In picture 2, they're on the table.

Picture 1

Picture 2

GROUP WORK Describe the people in the pictures. Don't say the person's name.
Your classmates guess the person.

A: He's wearing blue jeans, a beige shirt, and a black jacket. Who is it?

B: Is it John Cho?

A: No, it isn't.

B: Is it Liam Hemsworth?

A: That's right.

Bradley Cooper

Rashida Jones

Neymar

Cristiano Ronaldo

Idris Elba

Scarlett Johansson

Ariana Grande

John Cho

Ang Lee

Kate Middleton

Zoe Saldana

Liam Hemsworth

INTERCHANGE 3 Let's talk!

A CLASS ACTIVITY Talk to your classmates. Ask two different classmates each question. Write their names and answers.

Question	Name:	Name:
What's your last name?		
Where are you from?		
What is your parents' first language?		
How do you spell your best friend's name?		
What's your best friend like?		
What is your email address?		
What is your phone number?		

B CLASS ACTIVITY Tell the class two things about your partners.

"Yumi's last name is Suzuki. Francisco is from Guatemala."

What's wrong with this picture?

GROUP WORK What's wrong with this picture? Tell your classmates.

"Mia and Karen are playing basketball, but they're wearing dresses!"

A CLASS ACTIVITY Go around the class and find this information.
Try to write a different name on each line.

Find someone who ...

	Name
gets up at 5:00 A.M. on weekdays	
gets up at noon on Saturdays	
does homework on Sunday night	
works at night	
works on weekends	
has a pet	
dances on Friday night	
lives alone	
takes a bus to class	
rides a motorcycle to class	
cooks on weekends	
plays the drums	
has two brothers	
writes emails every day	
speaks three languages	
doesn't eat breakfast	

work at night

cook on the weekends

play the drums

A: Do you get up at 5:00 A.M. on weekdays, Kun-woo?
B: No, I get up at six-thirty.
A: Do you get up at 5:00 A.M. on weekdays, Yasmin?
C: Yes, I get up at 5:00 A.M. every day.

B GROUP WORK Compare your answers.

A: Kun-woo gets up at six-thirty on weekdays.
B: Yasmin gets up at 5:00 on weekdays.
C: Lucas gets up at . . .

A **PAIR WORK** Find the differences between Tony's apartment and Nicole's apartment.

Tony's apartment

Nicole's apartment

    A: There are four chairs in Tony's kitchen, but there are three chairs in Nicole's kitchen.
    B: There is a sofa in Tony's living room, but there is no sofa in Nicole's living room.

B **GROUP WORK** Compare your answers.

A PAIR WORK Imagine you're looking for a job. What do you want to do? First, check (✓) your answers to the questions. Then ask your partner the same questions.

	Me		My partner	
Do you want to . . . ?	Yes	No	Yes	No
work from 9 to 5	☐	☐	☐	☐
work in an office	☐	☐	☐	☐
work outdoors	☐	☐	☐	☐
work at home	☐	☐	☐	☐
work with a team	☐	☐	☐	☐
use a computer	☐	☐	☐	☐
use English	☐	☐	☐	☐
travel	☐	☐	☐	☐
talk to people	☐	☐	☐	☐
help people	☐	☐	☐	☐
wear a suit	☐	☐	☐	☐
perform in front of people	☐	☐	☐	☐

work from 9 to 5

perform in front of people

work outdoors

work with a team

Positive	**Negative**
It's easy. / It's an easy job.	It's difficult. / It's a difficult job.
It's exciting. / It's an exciting job.	It's boring. / It's a boring job.
It's terrific. / It's a terrific job.	It's very stressful. / It's a very stressful job.
It's pretty relaxing. / It's a pretty relaxing job.	It's really dangerous. / It's a really dangerous job.

B PAIR WORK Think of a good job for your partner. Go to pages 50 and 53 for ideas.

A: You want to travel and use English. Do you want to be a pilot?

B: No, a pilot's job is very stressful.

A: OK, do you want to be . . . ?

This page is intentionally left blank

Grammar plus

1 My, your, his, her page 3

■ Use *his* with males and *her* with females: **His** name is Travis. (NOT: ~~Her name is Travis.~~)
Her name is Nicole. (NOT: ~~His name is Nicole.~~)

Complete the conversations with *my*, *your*, *his*, or *her*.

1. A: Hello. _____My_____ name is Carlos.

　　B: Hi, Carlos. What's _____ last name?

　　A: It's Gonzales.

　　B: How do you spell _____ last name? Is it G-O-N-Z-A-L-E-Z?

　　A: No, it's G-O-N-Z-A-L-E-S. And what's _____ name?

　　B: _____ name is Bill Powers. Nice to meet you.

2. A: What's Ms. Robinson's first name?

　　B: _____ first name is Elizabeth. _____ nickname is Liz.

　　A: I'm sorry. What's _____ first name again?

　　B: It's Elizabeth. And what's Mr. Weber's first name?

　　A: _____ first name is Peter.

　　B: That's right. And _____ nickname is Pete.

　　A: That's right, too!

2 The verb *be* page 5

■ In questions, the verb *be* comes before the noun or pronoun: **Are you** Joshua Brown?
Is he in our English class? **Is she** the teacher?

■ Don't use contractions in short answers with *Yes*: Are you in my class?
Yes, **I am**. (NOT: ~~Yes, I'm.~~)

Complete the conversations with the words in the box.

am	I'm	it's	she's	you're
✓ are	I am	I'm not	you	

1. A: Excuse me. _____Are_____ you Layla Moore?

　　B: No, _____. _____ over there.

　　A: OK. Thanks.

2. A: Hi. Are _____ Layla Moore?

　　B: Yes, _____.

　　A: Nice to meet you. _____ Sergio Oliveira.
　　_____ in my English class.

　　B: Yes, I _____. _____ nice to meet you too, Sergio.

1 *This/these; it/they;* plurals page 10

- Don't use a contraction with *What* + *are*: **What** are these? (NOT: ~~What're these?~~)
- Use *this* with singular nouns: **This** is a laptop. Use *these* with plural nouns: **These** are flash drives.

Choose the correct words.

1. A: What's / (**What are**) **these?**
   B: It's / They're my **flash drive / flash drives**.

2. A: What's / What are this?
   B: It's / They're a / an cell phone.

3. A: What's this / these?
   B: It's / They're a / an English book.

2 Yes/No and *where* questions with *be* page 11

- In questions with *where*, the verb comes after *Where*: **Where** is my credit card?
  (NOT: ~~Where my credit card is?~~) **Where** are my sunglasses? (NOT: ~~Where my sunglasses are?~~)

A Match the questions with the answers.

1. Is that your wallet? __*c*__   **a.** They're in your backpack.
2. Are these your glasses? _____   **b.** No, it's not.
3. Where are my keys? _____   **c.** Oh, yes, it is!
4. Is this your bicycle? _____   **d.** It's on my desk.
5. Where's your tablet? _____   **e.** No, they're not.

B Complete the conversation. Use the words in the box.

are they	it is	they are	where
it	it's	this	✓ where's

A: ____Where's____ my dictionary?
B: I don't know. Is _____ in your backpack?
A: No, _____ not.
B: Is _____ your dictionary?
A: Yes, _____ Thanks! Now, _____ are my glasses?
B: _____ on your desk?
A: Yes, _____. Thank you!

UNIT 3

1 Negative statements and yes/no questions with *be* page 17

■ Use *be* + *not* to form negative statements: Ana **isn't** a student. (NOT: ~~Ana no is a student.~~)

■ *You* is a singular and a plural pronoun: Are **you** from Rio? Yes, **I** am./Yes, **we** are.

A Unscramble the words to write negative statements.

1. is / of Canada / Toronto / the capital / not
   Toronto is not the capital of Canada.

2. Buenos Aires / not / from / we're
   _____

3. not / you and Ashley / in my class / are
   _____

4. is / my first language / Korean / not
   _____

5. from / my mother / not / is / Italy
   _____

6. my parents / not / are / they
   _____

B Complete the conversations.

1. **A:** _____Are_____ you and your friend from Costa Rica?
   B: No, _____ not. _____ from the Dominican Republic.

2. **A:** _____ your first language Spanish?
   B: Yes, it _____. My parents _____ from Ecuador.

3. **A:** _____ Nadia and Rayan Lebanese?
   B: Yes, _____ are. But _____in France now.

4. **A:** _____ my friends and I late?
   B: No, _____ not. _____ early!

2 Wh-questions with *be* page 20

■ Use *what* to ask about things. Use *where* to ask about places. Use *who* to ask about people. Use *What is/are . . . like?* to ask for a description.

■ Use *how* to ask for a description: **How are** you today? Use *how old* to ask about age: **How old** is he?

■ In answers about age, you can use only the number or the number + years old: He's **18**. OR He's **18 years old**. (NOT: ~~He has 18 years.~~)

Complete the questions with *how*, *what*, *where*, or *who*. Then match the questions with the answers.

1. _Who_ is that? _d_
2. _____ is her name? _____
3. _____ is she like? _____
4. _____ old is she? _____
5. _____ your family from? _____
6. _____ is Kyoto like? _____

a. We're from Japan – from Kyoto.
b. She's 18.
c. Her name is Hina.
d. She's my sister.
e. Oh, it's really beautiful.
f. She's very nice and friendly.

1 Possessives *page 24*

> ■ The noun comes after a possessive adjective: This is **my** T-shirt.
>
> ■ Don't include the noun after a possessive pronoun: This T-shirt is **mine**.
>
> ■ *Whose* can be used with singular and plural nouns: **Whose** scarf is this? **Whose** sneakers are these?

Complete the conversations. Use the words in the boxes. There are two extra words in each box.

his	mine	my	your	yours	✓ whose

1. A: _____Whose_____ jacket is this? Is it _____, Ethan?

   B: No, it's not _____. Ask Matt. I think it's _____.

her	my	mine	your	yours

2. A: These aren't _____ gloves. Are they _____?

   B: No, they're not _____. Maybe they are Young-min's.

her	hers	their	theirs	whose

3. A: _____ sweaters are these? Are they Rachel's?

   B: No, they're not _____ sweaters. But these shorts are _____.

2 Present continuous statements; conjunctions *page 26*

> ■ The present continuous is the present of *be* + verb + -*ing*: It**'s raining**. She**'s wearing** a raincoat.
>
> ■ The two negative contractions mean the same: **He's not/He isn't** wearing a coat.
> **We're not/We aren't** wearing gloves.

Change the affirmative sentences to negative sentences. Change the negative sentences to affirmative sentences.

1. Mr. and Mrs. Liu are wearing green caps. _____Mr. and Mrs. Liu aren't wearing green caps._____

2. It isn't snowing. _____

3. I'm wearing a winter coat. _____

4. You're wearing David's sunglasses. _____

5. Ayumi isn't wearing a scarf. _____

3 Present continuous yes/no questions; adjective + noun *page 27*

> ■ In questions, the present continuous is *be* + subject + verb + –*ing*: **Is** it **raining**? **Are** you **wearing** a raincoat?
>
> ■ Adjectives can come before nouns or after the verb *be*: He's wearing **a blue hat**. His hat **is blue**.
>
> ■ Adjectives don't have a plural form: a **green hat**; two **green hats**.

Write questions using the words in parentheses. Then complete the responses.

1. A. _Is Mr. Thomas wearing a dark blue coat?_ (wear, dark blue coat)

   B: No, he _____.

2. A: _____ (wear, high heels)

   B: No, we _____.

3. A: _____ (wear, a sweater)

   B: Yes, I _____.

4. A: _____ (rain)

   B: Yes, it _____.

1 **What time is it? / Is it A.M. or P.M.?** page 31

■ Remember: You can say times different ways: 1:15 = *one-fifteen* OR *a quarter after one.*

Write each sentence in a different way.

1. It's a quarter to four. <u>It's three forty-five.</u>
2. It's 7:00 P.M. <u>It's seven in the evening.</u>
3. It's six-fifteen. _____
4. It's 10 o'clock at night. _____
5. It's three-oh-five. _____
6. It's twenty-five to eleven. _____
7. It's one o'clock in the morning. _____
8. It's midnight. _____

2 **Present continuous Wh-questions** page 33

■ Use the present continuous to talk about actions that are happening right now:
What **are** you **doing**? **I'm talking** to you!
■ In questions, the *be* verb comes after the question word: What **are you** doing?
■ To form the continuous of verbs ending in –*e*, drop the *e* and add –*ing*: have → having.
■ For verbs ending in vowel + consonant, double the consonant and add –*ing*: get → getting.

What are the people doing? Write conversations. Use the words in parentheses.

1. A: <u>What's Matt doing?</u> (Matt)
   B: <u>He's swimming.</u> (swim)

2. A: _____ (Jon and Megan)
   B: _____ (shop)

3. A: _____ (you)
   B: _____ (write a message)

4. A: _____ (Chris)
   B: _____ (cook dinner)

5: A: _____ (you and Tyler)
   B: _____ (watch a movie)

6: A: _____ (Sara)
   B: _____ (have pizza)

7. A: _____ (you and Joseph)
   B: _____ (study for the test)

8. A: _____ (Laura and Paulo)
   B: _____ (chat online)

1 Simple present statements `page 37` **and Simple present statements with irregular verbs** `page 38`

> ■ In affirmative statements, verbs with *he/she/it* end in *–s*: He/She **walks** to school. BUT I/You/We/They **walk** to school.
>
> ■ In negative statements, use doesn't with *he/she/it* and don't with all the others: He/She/It **doesn't** live here. I/You/We/They **don't** live here.
>
> ■ Don't add *–s* to the verb: She **doesn't live** here. (NOT: ~~She doesn't lives here.~~)

Elena is talking about her family. Complete the sentences with the correct form of the verbs in parentheses.

My family and I _____live_____ (live) in the city. We _____ (have) an apartment on First Avenue. My sister _____ (go) to school near our apartment, so she _____ (walk) to school. My father _____ (work) in the suburbs, so he _____ (drive) to his job. My mother _____ (use) public transportation – she _____ (take) the bus to her office downtown. She _____ (have) a new job, but she _____ (not like) it very much. And me? Well, I _____ (not work) far from our apartment, so I _____ (not need) a car or public transportation. I _____ (ride) my bike to work!

2 Simple present questions `page 39`

> ■ In questions, use *does* with *he/she/it* and *do* with all the others: **Does** he/she/it get up early? **Do** I/you/we/they get up early?
>
> ■ Don't add *–s* to the verb: Does she **live** alone? (NOT: ~~Does she lives alone?~~)

A Write questions to complete the conversations.

1. **A:** _Do you use public transportation?_
   B: Yes, I use public transportation.

2. **A:** _____
   B: No, my family doesn't eat dinner at 5:00.

3. **A:** _____
   B: No, my brother doesn't take the bus to work.

4. **A:** _____
   B: No, I don't get up late on weekends.

> ■ Use *in* with *the morning/the afternoon/the evening*. Use *at* with *night*: I go to school **in** the afternoon and work **at** night.
>
> ■ Use *at* with clock times: She gets up **at** 8:00.
>
> ■ Use *on* with days: He sleeps late **on** weekends. She has class **on** Mondays.

B Complete the conversation with *at*, *in*, or *on*.

A: Does your family have breakfast together _____in_____ the morning?

B: Well, we eat together _____ weekends, but _____ weekdays we're all busy. My parents go to work early – _____ 6:30. But we eat dinner together _____ the evening, and we have a big lunch together _____ Sundays. We eat _____ noon. Then _____ the afternoon, we take a walk or go to the movies.

UNIT 7

1 Simple present short answers page 45

> ■ Remember: I/You/We/They **do/don't**. He/She/It **does/doesn't**.

Choose the correct words.

A: Do / (Does) your family **live / lives** in an apartment?

B: No, we **don't / doesn't**. We **have / has** a house.

A: That's nice. **Do / Does** your house have two floors?

B: Yes, it **do / does**. It **have / has** four rooms on the first floor. And we **have / has** three bedrooms and a bathroom on the second floor.

A: And **do / does** you and your family **have / has** a yard?

B: Yes, we **do / does**. And how about you, Tim? **Do / Does** you **live / lives** in a house, too?

A: No, I **don't / doesn't**. My wife and I **have / has** a small apartment in the city.

B: Oh. **Do / Does** you **like / likes** the city?

A: Yes, I **do / does**. But my wife **don't / doesn't**.

2 *There is, there are* page 47

> ■ Use *there is* with singular nouns: **There's** a bed. Use *there are* with plural nouns: **There are** two chairs.
> ■ Use *some* in affirmative statements: There are **some** chairs in the kitchen. Use *any* in negative statements: There aren't **any** chairs in the bedroom.

Read the information about the Perez family's new house. Write sentences with the phrases in the box.

there's a	there are some
there's no	there are no
there isn't a	there aren't any

1. A living room?	Yes.	
2. A dining room?	No.	
3. A microwave in the kitchen?	No.	
4. A table in the kitchen?	Yes.	
5. Curtains on the windows?	Yes.	
6. Rugs on the floors?	No.	
7. Closets in the bedrooms?	Yes.	
8. Bookcases in the bedrooms?	No.	

1. _There's a living room._

2. _____

3. _____

4. _____

5. _____

6. _____

7. _____

8. _____

1 Simple present Wh-questions page 52

> ■ Use *What* to ask about things: **What do** you do? Use *Where* to ask about places: **Where do** you work?
> Use *How do/does . . . like . . . ?* to ask for an opinion: **How does** he **like** his job?

Complete the conversations.

1. A: _What does your husband do_____?
   B: My husband? Oh, he's a nurse.
   A: Really? Where _____?
   B: He works at Mercy Hospital.

2. A: Where _____?
   B: I work in a restaurant.
   A: Nice! What _____?
   B: I'm a chef.

3. A: How _____?
   B: My job? I don't really like it very much.
   A: That's too bad. What _____?
   B: I'm a cashier. I work at a clothing store.

4. A: What _____?
   B: My brother is a doctor, and my sister is a lawyer.
   A: How _____?
   B: They work very hard, but they love their jobs.

2 Placement of adjectives page 54

> ■ Adjectives come after the verb *be*: A doctor's job **is stressful**. Adjectives come before nouns:
> A police officer has a **dangerous job**. (NOT: ~~A police officer has a job dangerous.~~)
> ■ Adjectives have the same form with singular or plural nouns: Firefighters and police officers have stressful
> jobs. (NOT: . . . have ~~stressfuls~~ jobs.)

Use the information to write two sentences.

1. accountant / job / boring
   An accountant's job is boring.
   An accountant has a boring job.

2. salesperson / job / stressful

   _____

   _____

3. security guard / job / dangerous

   _____

   _____

4. actor / job / exciting

   _____

   _____

5. host / job / interesting

   _____

   _____

6. nurse / job / difficult

   _____

   _____

Grammar plus answer key

Unit 1

1 *My, your, his, her*
1. A: Hello. **My** name is Carlos.
   B: Hi, Carlos. What's **your** last name?
   A: It's Gonzales.
   B: How do you spell **your** last name? Is it G-O-N-Z-A-L-E-Z?
   A: No, it's G-O-N-Z-A-L-E-S. And what's **your** name?
   B: **My** name is Bill Powers. Nice to meet you.
2. A: What's Ms. Robinson's first name?
   B: **Her** first name is Elizabeth. **Her** nickname is Liz.
   A: I'm sorry. What's **her** first name again?
   B: It's Elizabeth. And what's Mr. Weber's first name?
   A: **His** first name is Peter.
   B: That's right. And **his** nickname is Pete.
   A: That's right, too!

2 The verb *be*
1. A: Excuse me. **Are** you Layla Moore?

   B: No, **I'm not**. **She's** over there.
   A: OK. Thanks.
2. A: Hi. Are **you** Layla Moore?
   B: Yes, **I am**.
   A: Nice to meet you. **I'm** Sergio Oliveira. **You're** in my English class.
   B: Yes, I **am**. **It's** nice to meet you too, Sergio.

Unit 2

1 *This/These; it/they; plurals*
1. A: **What are** these?
   B: **They're** my flash drives.
2. A: **What's** this?
   B: **It's** a cell phone.
3. A: What's **this**?
   B: **It's an** English book.

2 Yes/No and *where* questions with *be*
A
1. c   2. e   3. a   4. b   5. d

B
A: **Where's** my dictionary?
B: I don't know. Is **it** in your backpack?
A: No, **it's** not.
B: Is **this** your dictionary?
A: Yes, **it** is. Thanks! Now, where **are** my glasses?
B: **Are** they on your desk?
A: Yes, **they are**. Thank you!

Unit 3

1 Negative statements and yes/no questions with *be*
A
2. We're not from Buenos Aires.
3. You and Ashley are not in my class.
4. My first language is not Korean. / Korean is not my first language.
5. My mother is not from Italy.
6. They are not my parents.

B
1. B: No, **are** not. **We're/We are** from the Dominican Republic.
2. A: **Is** your first language Spanish?
   B: Yes, it **is**. My parents **are** from Ecuador.
3. A: **Are** Nadia and Rayan Lebanese?
   B: Yes, **they** are. But **they're/they are** in France now.
4. A: **Are** my friends and I late?
   B: No, **you're/you are** not. **You're/You are** early!

2 Wh-questions with *be*
2. **What** is her name?   c
3. **What** is she like?   f
4. **How** old is she?   b
5. **Where** is your family from?   a
6. **What** is Kyoto like?   e

Unit 4

1 Possessives
1. A: **Whose** jacket is this? Is it **yours**, Ethan?
   B: No, it's not **mine**. Ask Matt. I think it's **his**.
2. A: These aren't **my** gloves. Are they **yours**?
   B: No, they're not **mine.** Maybe they are Young-min's.
3. A: **Whose** sweaters are these? Are they Rachel's?
   B: No, they're not **her** sweaters. But these shorts are **hers**.

2 Present continuous statements; conjunctions
2. It's snowing.
3. I'm not wearing a winter coat.
4. You're not/You aren't wearing David's sunglasses.
5. Ayumi is wearing a scarf.

3 Present continuous yes/no questions
1. B: No, **he's not/he isn't.**
2. A: **Are you wearing** high heels?
   B: No, **we're not/we aren't.**
3. A: **Are you wearing** a sweater?
   B: Yes, **I am**.
4. A: **Is it** raining?
   B: Yes, **it is.**

Unit 5

1 What time is it? / Is it A.M. or P.M.?
3. It's a quarter after six.
4. It's 10:00 P.M.
5. It's five (minutes) after three.
6. It's ten thirty-five.
7. It's one A.M.
8. It's 12:00 A.M./It's twelve (o'clock) at night.

2 Present continuous Wh-questions
2. A: What are Jon and Megan doing?
   B: They're shopping.
3. A: What are you doing?
   B: I'm writing a message.
4. A: What's Chris doing?
   B: He's cooking dinner.
5. A: What are you and Tyler doing?
   B: We're watching a movie.
6. A: What's Sara doing?
   B: She's having pizza.
7. A: What are you and Joseph doing?
   B: We're studying for a test.
8. A: What are Laura and Paulo doing?
   B: They're chatting online.

Unit 6

1 Simple present statements and Simple present statements with irregular verbs
My family and I **live** in the city. We **have** an apartment on First Avenue. My sister **goes** to school near our apartment, so she **walks** to school. My father **works** in the suburbs, so he **drives** to his job. My mother **uses** public transportation – she **takes** the bus to her office downtown. She **has** a new job, but she **doesn't like** it very much. And me? Well, I **don't work** far from our apartment, so I **don't need** a car or public transportation. I **ride** my bike to work!

2 Simple present questions
A
2. A: Does your family eat dinner at 5:00?
3. A: Does your brother take the bus to work?
4. A: Do you get up late on weekends?

B
B: Well, we eat together **on** weekends, but **on** weekdays we're all busy. My parents go to work early – **at** 6:30. But we eat dinner together **in** the evening, and we have a big lunch together **on** Sundays. We eat **at** noon. Then **in** the afternoon, we take a walk or go to the movies.

Unit 7

1 Simple present short answers
A: **Does** your family **live** in an apartment?
B: No, we **don't**. We **have** a house.
A: That's nice. **Does** your house have two floors?
B: Yes, it **does**. It **has** four rooms on the first floor. And we **have** three bedrooms and a bathroom on the second floor.
A: And **do** you and your family **have** a yard?
B: Yes, we **do**. And how about you, Tim? **Do** you **live** in a house, too?
A: No, I **don't**. My wife and I **have** a small apartment in the city.
B: Oh. **Do** you **like** the city?
A: Yes, I **do**. But my wife **doesn't**.

2 *There is, there are*
2. There's no / There isn't a dining room.
3. There's no / There isn't a microwave in the kitchen.
4. There's a table in the kitchen.
5. There are some curtains on the windows.
6. There are no / There aren't any rugs on the floors.
7. There are closets in the bedrooms.
8. There are no / There aren't any bookcases in the bedroom.

Unit 8

1 Simple present Wh-questions
1. A: Really? Where **does he work**?
2. A: Where **do you work**?
   B: I work in a restaurant.
   A: Nice! What **do you do**?
   B: I'm a chef.
3. A: How **do you like your job**?
   B: My job? I don't really like it very much.
   A: That's too bad. What **do you do**?
   B: I'm a cashier. I work at a clothing store.
4. A: What **do your brother and sister do**?
   B: My brother is a doctor, and my sister is a lawyer.
   A: How **do they like their jobs**?
   B: They work very hard, but they love their jobs.

2 Placement of adjectives
2. A salesperson's job is stressful.
   A salesperson has a stressful job.
3. A security guard's job is dangerous.
   A security guard has a dangerous job.
4. An actor's job is exciting.
   An actor has an exciting job.
5. A host's job is interesting.
   A host has an interesting job.
6. A nurse's job is difficult.
   A nurse has a difficult job.

Credits

The authors and publishers acknowledge the following sources of copyright material and are grateful for the permissions granted. While every effort has been made, it has not always been possible to identify the sources of all the material used, or to trace all copyright holders. If any omissions are brought to our notice, we will be happy to include the appropriate acknowledgements on reprinting and in the next update to the digital edition, as applicable.

Texts

The Roxbury for the adapted text on p. 49. Reproduced with kind permission; Attrap'Rêves for the adapted text on p. 49. Reproduced with kind permission.

Key: B = Below, BL = Below Left, BC = Below Centre, BR = Below Right, B/G = Background, C = Centre, CL = Centre Left, CR = Centre Right, Ex = Exercise, TC = Top Centre, T = Top, TL = Top Left, TR = Top Right.

Illustrations

337 Jon (KJA Artists): 24, 29, 85; **Mark Duffin**: 15, 12(T), 31(T), 44(T), 47, 115, 121; **Thomas Girard** (Good Illustration): 3, 11, 13, 23, 25, 36, 37, 50, 79(T), 89, 100, 102; **Dusan Lakicevic** (Beehive Illustration): 21, 41, 87; **Quino Marin** (The Organisation): 26, 31(B), 79(B); **Gavin Reece** (New Division): 27, 44(B), 45, 101; **Gary Venn** (Lemonade Illustration): 56, 88, 90, 91, 127, 128; **Paul Williams** (Sylvie Poggio Artists): 9, 30, 119.

Photos

Back cover (woman with whiteboard): Jenny Acheson/Stockbyte/GettyImages; Back cover (whiteboard): Nemida/GettyImages; Back cover (man using phone): Betsie Van Der Meer/Taxi/GettyImages; Back cover (woman smiling): PeopleImages.com/DigitalVision/GettyImages; Back cover (name tag): Tetra Images/GettyImages; Back cover (handshake): David Lees/Taxi/GettyImages; p. v: PhotoAlto/Sigrid Olsson/PhotoAlto Agency RF Collections/GettyImages; p. 2 (header), p. vi (unit 1): Paul Bradbury/OJO Images; p. 2 (CR): Paul Bradbury/Caiaimage/GettyImages; p. 2 (BL): Stefania D'Alessandro/WireImage/GettyImages; p. 2 (BR): Steve Granitz/WireImage/GettyImages; p. 4 (Ex 7.1): Maskot/Maskot/GettyImages; p. 4 (Ex 7.2): Design Pics/Ron Nickel/GettyImages; p. 4 (Ex 7.3): Dan Dalton/Caiaimage/GettyImages; p. 4 (Ex 7.4): Squaredpixels/E+/GettyImages; p. 5 (T): Fabrice LEROUGE/ONOKY/GettyImages; p. 5 (C): Erik Dreyer/The Image Bank/GettyImages; p. 5 (B): theboone/E+/GettyImages; p. 6: Maskot/Maskot/GettyImages; p. 7 (T): Peter Dazeley/Photographer's Choice/GettyImages; p. 7 (Ex 14.1): Tim Robberts/The Image Bank/GettyImages; p. 7 (Ex 14.2): Klaus Vedfelt/DigitalVision/GettyImages; p. 7 (Ex 14.3): Nicolas McComber/E+/GettyImages; p. 7 (Ex 14.4): Ariel Skelley/Blend Images/GettyImages; p. 8 (header), p. vi (unit 2): John Slater/Stockbyte/GettyImages; p. 8 (backpack): igor terekhov/iStock/GettyImagesPlus; p. 8 (cellphone): Peter Dazeley/Photographer's Choice/GettyImages; p. 8 (hairbrush): slobo/E+/GettyImages; p. 8 (sunglasses): Fodor90/iStock/GettyImages; p. 8 (wallet): bibikoff/E+/GettyImages; p. 8 (keys): Floortje/E+/GettyImages; p. 8 (umbrella): Picheat Suviyanond/iStock/GettyImages; p. 8 (energy bar): Juanmonino/iStock/Getty Images Plus/GettyImages; p. 8 (book): Image Source/Image Source/GettyImages; p. 8 (notebook): kyoshino/E+/GettyImages; p. 8 (pen): Ann Flanigan/EyeEm/Fuse/GettyImages; p. 8 (eraser): subjug/iStock/GettyImages; p. 8 (clock): GoodGnom/DigitalVision Vectors/GettyImages; p. 9 (tablet): daboost/iStock/Getty Images Plus/GettyImages; p. 9 (box): Guy Crittenden/Photographer's Choice/GettyImages; p. 9 (phone case): Jeffrey Coolidge/DigitalVision/GettyImages; p. 9 (television): Cobalt88/iStock/GettyImages; p. 9 (newspaper): -Oxford-/E+/GettyImages; p. 9 (Id): Daniel Ernst/iStock/Getty Images Plus/GettyImages; p. 9 (clip): Steven von Niederhausern/E+/GettyImages; p. 9 (ticket): Gediminas Zalgevicius/Hemera/GettyImages; p. 9 (purse): Stramyk/iStock/GettyImages; p. 10 (flash drive): zentilia/iStock/Getty Images Plus/GettyImages; p. 10 (laptop): Coprid/iStock/Getty Images Plus/GettyImages; p. 10 (laptops.): karandaev/iStock/GettyImages; p. 10 (keys): krungchingpixs/iStock/GettyImages; p. 10 (backpacks): pavila/iStock/GettyImages; p. 10 (umbrella): Kais Tolmats/E+/GettyImages; p. 10 (sunglasses): Zaharia_Bogdan/iStock/GettyImages; p. 10 (wallet): malerapaso/iStock/GettyImages; p. 10 (window): beright/iStock/GettyImages; p. 10 (credit card): freestylephoto/iStock/GettyImages; p. 10 (headphones): tiler84/iStock/GettyImages; p. 12 (backpack): JulNichols/E+/GettyImages; p. 12 (flash drive): Garsya/iStock/GettyImages; p. 12 (laptop): Creative Crop/Photodisc/GettyImages; p. 12 (newspaper): goir/iStock/GettyImages; p. 12 (computer): AlexLMX/iStock/GettyImages; p. 12 (chair): urfinguss/iStock/GettyImages; p. 12 (wallet): pioneer111/iStock/GettyImages; p. 12 (notebook): drpnncpp/iStock/GettyImages; p. 12 (tv): selensergen/iStock/GettyImages; p. 12 (glasses): bonetta/iStock/GettyImages; p. 15 (cellphone): Manuel Faba Ortega/iStock/GettyImages; p. 15 (cellphones): sunnycircle/iStock/GettyImages; p. 15 (purse): penguenstok/E+/GettyImages; p. 15 (purses): iulianvalentin/iStock/GettyImages; p. 15 (wallet): Nyo09/iStock/GettyImages; p. 15 (wallets): alarich/iStock/GettyImages; p. 16 (header), p. vi (unit 3): stock_colors/iStock/Getty Images Plus/GettyImages; p. 16 (T): Photography by ZhangXun/Moment/GettyImages; p. 16 (BL): Roberto Westbrook/Blend Images/GettyImages; p. 17 (T): Robert Frerck/The Image Bank/GettyImages; p. 17 (B): Jane Sweeney/The Image Bank/GettyImages; p. 18 (Ex 5.1): Dan MacMedan/WireImage/GettyImages; p. 18 (Ex 5.2): Steve Granitz/WireImage/GettyImages; p. 18 (Ex 5.3): Clasos/CON/LatinContent Editorial/GettyImages; p. 18 (Ex 5.4): Koki Nagahama/Getty Images AsiaPac/GettyImages; p. 18 (Ex 5.5): Jeff Spicer/Getty Images Entertainment/GettyImages; p. 19 (TR): SolStock/E+/GettyImages; p. 19 (cellphone): Peter Dazeley/Photographer's Choice/GettyImages; p. 19 (Ben): Hero Images/Hero Images/GettyImage; p. 19 (Nadia): Portra Images/DigitalVision/GettyImages; p. 19 (Ex 7.c.a): Fuse/Corbis/GettyImages; p. 19 (Ex 7.c.b): Purestock/GettyImages; p. 19 (Ex 7.c.c): Lucy Lambriex/Moment/GettyImages; p. 19 (Ex 7.c.d): James Woodson/Photodisc/GettyImages; p. 19 (Ex 7.c.e): Fuse/Corbis/GettyImages; p. 20 (Ex 8.a.1): Alex Barlow/Moment/GettyImages; p. 20 (Ex 8.a.2): Jupiterimages/Stockbyte/GettyImages; p. 20 (Ex 8.a.3): PhotoAlto/Frederic Cirou/PhotoAlto Agency RF Collections/GettyImages; p. 20 (Ex 8.a.4): Hill Street Studios/Blend Images/GettyImages; p. 22 (header), p. vi (unit 4): Sam Edwards/Caiaimage/GettyImages; p. 22 (formal man): Spiderstock/E+/GettyImages; p. 22 (formal woman): Grady Reese/E+/GettyImages; p. 22 (rain coat): EdnaM/iStock/Getty Images Plus/GettyImages; p. 22 (coat): DonNichols/E+/GettyImages; p. 22 (dress): ARSELA/E+/GettyImages; p. 22 (casual woman): BLOOM image/BLOOMimage/GettyImages; p. 22 (pajamas): madtwinsis/E+/GettyImages; p. 22 (swimwear): dendong/iStock/Getty Images Plus/GettyImages; p. 22 (shorts): 487387674/iStock/Getty Images Plus/GettyImages; p. 22 (cap): Steve Zmina/DigitalVision Vectors/GettyImages; p. 25 (brazilian flag): Image Source/Image Source/GettyImages; p. 25 (japanese flag): Jim Ballard/Photographer's Choice/GettyImages; p. 25 (american flag): NirdalArt/iStock/GettyImages; p. 25 (canadian flag): Encyclopaedia Britannica/UIG/Universal Images Group/GettyImages; p. 25 (TL): Andrea Pistolesi/Photolibrary/GettyImages; p. 25 (TR): Photograph by Kangheewan/Moment Open/GettyImages; p. 25 (BL): Bruce Leighty/Photolibrary/GettyImages; p. 25 (BR): EschCollection/Photonica/GettyImages; p. 25 (thermometer): Burke/Triolo Productions/Stockbyte/GettyImages; p. 29: PeopleImages.com/DigitalVision/GettyImages; p. 30 (header), p. vi (unit 5): Driendl Group/Photographer's Choice/GettyImages; p. 30 (Brian): Daniel Grill/GettyImages; p. 30 (Amar): Peter Cade/The Image Bank/GettyImages; p. 31 (Ex 3.a.1): Raimund Koch/The Image Bank/GettyImages; p. 31 (Ex 3.a.2): Science Photo Library/Science Photo Library/GettyImages; p. 31 (Ex 3.a.3): Paul Bricknell/Dorling Kindersley/GettyImages; p. 31 (Ex 3.a.4): SergeiKorolko/iStock/GettyImages; p. 31 (Ex 3.a.5): pagadesign/iStock/GettyImages; p. 31 (Ex 3.a.6): scanrail/iStock/GettyImages; p. 32 (T): Plume Creative/DigitalVision/GettyImages; p. 32 (BR): B. Sporrer/J.Skowronek/StockFood Creative/GettyImages; p. 32 (Jay): B. Sporrer/J.Skowronek/StockFood Creative/GettyImages; p. 32 (Kate): Rafael Elias/Moment Open/GettyImages; p. 33 (TL): Tetra Images/Brand X Pictures/GettyImages; p. 33 (TC): Hola Images/GettyImages; p. 33 (TR): Tim Robberts/The Image Bank; p. 33 (CL): annebaek/iStock/Getty Images Plus/GettyImages; p. 33 (C): Stockbyte/Stockbyte/GettyImages; p. 33 (CR): Caiaimage/Tom Merton/Caiaimage/GettyImages; p. 33 (BL): LWA/Sharie Kennedy/Blend Images/GettyImages; p. 33 (BC): sot/DigitalVision/GettyImages; p. 33 (BR): David Crunelle/EyeEm/EyeEm/GettyImages; p. 34 (dance): Blend Images - Ariel Skelley/GettyImages; p. 34 (drive): Westend61/Westend61/GettyImages; p. 34 (music): Hero Images/Hero Images/GettyImages; p. 34 (basketball): Daniel Grill/Tetra images/GettyImages; p. 34 (read): Peathegee Inc/Blend Images/GettyImages; p. 34 (bycycle): Daniel Milchev/The Image Bank/GettyImages; p. 34 (run): Ty Milford/Aurora Open/GettyImages; p. 34 (shop): BJI/Blue Jean Images/blue jean images/GettyImages; p. 34 (study): JAG IMAGES/DigitalVision/GettyImages; p. 34 (swim): J J D/Cultura/GettyImages; p. 34 (walk): Dougal Waters/Photographer's Choice RF/GettyImages; p. 34 (movie): Blend Images/Andres Rodriguez/Blend Images/GettyImages; p. 35 (Eva35): Sebastian Doerken/fStop/GettyImages; p. 35 (PamL): Denis Schneider/EyeEm/EyeEm/GettyImages; p. 35 (TL): Hero Images/Hero Images/GettyImages; p. 35 (BR): Betsie Van Der Meer/Taxi/GettyImages; p. 36 (header), p. vi (unit 6): Enrique Díaz/7cero/Moment/GettyImages; p. 36 (Ex 1.1): Image Source/DigitalVision/GettyImages; p. 36 (Ex 1.2): Kentaroo Tryman/Maskot/GettyImages; p. 36 (Ex 1.3): Susanne Kronholm/Johner Images Royalty-Free/GettyImages; p. 36 (Ex 1.4): Eternity in an Instant/The Image Bank/GettyImages; p. 36 (Ex 1.5): Marilyn Nieves/iStock/GettyImages; p. 36 (Ex 1.6): Matt Dutile/Image Source/GettyImages; p. 36 (Ex 1.7): Ciaran Griffin/Stockbyte/GettyImages; p. 36 (Ex 1.8): Maria Teijeiro/DigitalVision/GettyImages; p. 38: Robert Daly/Caiaimage/GettyImages; p. 39: Michael Berman/DigitalVision/GettyImages; p. 40: Frank van Delft/Cultura/GettyImages; p. 41: vadimguzhva/iStock/GettyImages; p. 42 (man): James Whitaker/DigitalVision/GettyImages; p. 42 (woman): Tyler Stableford/The Image Bank/GettyImage; p. 43: Pingebat/DigitalVision Vectors; p. 44 (header), p. vi (unit 7): Peter Adams/Photolibrary; p. 45 (lobby): piovesempre/iStock/GettyImages; p. 45 (apartment): Joe_Potato/iStock/GettyImages; p. 45 (house): Ron Evans/Photolibrary/GettyImages; p. 45 (kitchen): ttatty/iStock/GettyImages; p. 46 (armchair): xiaoke ma/E+/GettyImages; p. 46 (stove): taist/iStock/GettyImages; p. 46 (curtains): darksite/iStock/GettyImages; p. 46 (pictures): Glow Decor/Glow/GettyImages; p. 46 (bed): Emevil/iStock/GettyImages; p. 46 (coffee maker): GeorgePeters/E+/GettyImages; p. 46 (table): EdnaM/iStock/GettyImages; p. 46 (coffee table): DonNichols/E+/GettyImages; p. 46 (oven): mbbirdy/E+/GettyImages; p. 46 (refrigerator): JazzIRT/E+/GettyImages; p. 46 (lamps1): Creative Crop/DigitalVision/GettyImages; p. 46 (lamps2): stuartbur/E+/GettyImages; p. 46 (sofa): AnnaDavy/iStock/GettyImages; p. 46 (desk): Hemera Technologies/PhotoObjects.net/GettyImages; p. 46 (bookcase): DonNichols/iStock/GettyImages; p. 46 (dresser): Hemera Technologies/PhotoObjects.net/GettyImages; p. 46 (chairs): Firmafotografen/iStock/Getty Images Plus/GettyImages; p. 46 (mirror): Omer Yurdakul Gundogdu/E+/GettyImages; p. 46 (rug): DEA/G. CIGOLINI/De Agostini Picture Library/GettyImages; p. 46 (cupboards): ChoochartSansong/iStock/GettyImages; p. 47: Marco Baass/GettyImages; p. 48 (loft): Martin Barraud/OJO Images/GettyImages; p. 48 (mountains): Barrett & MacKay/All Canada Photos/GettyImages; p. 48 (villa): Maremagnum/Photolibrary/GettyImages; p. 48 (beach house): catnap72/E+/GettyImages; p. 49 (T): BERTHIER Emmanuel/hemis.fr/hemis.fr/GettyImages; p. 49 (B): Michael Marquand/Lonely Planet Images/GettyImages; p. 50 (header), p. vi (unit 8): iStock/Getty Images Plus/GettyImages; p. 51 (hospital): Vincent Hazat/PhotoAlto Agency RF Collections/GettyImages; p. 51 (office): Peopleimages/E+/GettyImages; p. 51 (store): Maskot/Maskot/GettyImages; p. 51 (hotel): DAJ/amana images/GettyImages; p. 51 (BR): Nevena1987/iStock/GettyImages; p. 51 (Jorden): Sam Edwards/OJO Images/GettyImages; p. 51 (Alicia): Philipp Nemenz/Cultura/GettyImages; p. 52 (BL): Digital Vision./DigitalVision/GettyImages; p. 52 (BC): PeopleImages/DigitalVision/GettyImages; p. 52 (BR): Glow Images, Inc/Glow/GettyImages; p. 53 (lawyer): rubberball/GettyImages; p. 53 (pilot): Katja Kircher/Maskot/GettyImages; p. 53 (photographer): stock_colors/E+/GettyImages; p. 53 (engineer): Thomas Barwick/Iconica/GettyImages; p. 53 (BR): Rubberball/Mike Kemp/Brand X Pictures/GettyImages; p. 53 (Paula): Marc Romanelli/Blend Images/GettyImages; p. 54 (T): Hero Images/Hero Images/GettyImages; p. 54 (B): Jetta Productions/Stone/GettyImages; p. 55 (B): Australian Scenics/Photolibrary/GettyImages; p. 55 (T): Eugenio Marongiu/Cultura/GettyImages; p. 57 (veterinarian): fotoedu/iStock/GettyImages; p. 57 (dentist): XiXinXing/XiXinXing/GettyImages; p. 57 (architect): John Lund/Marc Romanelli/Blend Images/GettyImages; p. 57 (hairstylst): Glow Images, Inc/Glow/GettyImages; p. 114 (CR): Pascal Le Segretain/Getty Images Entertainment/GettyImages; p. 114 (BR): Amanda Edwards/WireImage/GettyImages; p. 116 (Bradley Cooper): Steve Granitz/WireImage/GettyImages; p. 116 (Rashida Jones): Stefanie Keenan/WireImage/GettyImages; p. 116 (Neymar): David Ramos/Getty Images; p. 116 (Ronaldo): Anthony Harvey/Getty Images Entertainment/GettyImages; p. 116 (Idris Elba): Dave J Hogan/Getty Images Entertainment/GettyImages; p. 116 (Scarlett Johansson): Ray Tamarra/WireImage/GettyImages; p. 117 (Ariana Grande): Christopher Polk/Getty Images Entertainment/GettyImages; p. 117 (John Cho): John M. Heller/Getty Images Entertainment/GettyImages; p. 117 (Ang Lee): Pascal Le Segretain/Getty Images Entertainment/GettyImages; p. 117 (Kate Middleton): Anwar Hussein/WireImage/GettyImages; p. 117 (Zoe Saldana): Jon Kopaloff/FilmMagic/GettyImages; p. 117 (Liam Hemsworth): Joe Scarnici/Getty Images Entertainment/GettyImages; p. 118: PeopleImages.com/DigitalVision/GettyImages; p. 120 (TR): Garry Wade/The Image Bank/GettyImages; p. 120 (CR): Indeed/ABSODELS/GettyImages; p. 120 (BR): Joos Mind/Photographer's Choice/GettyImages; p. 122 (CR): urbancow/iStock/GettyImages; p. 122 (TR): George Doyle/Stockbyte/GettyImages; p. 122 (BL): Dennis K. Johnson/Lonely Planet Images/GettyImages; p. 122 (BR): baona/E+/GettyImages

interchange

FIFTH EDITION

Video Activity
Worksheets

intro A

Jack C. Richards
Revised by Karen Davy

CAMBRIDGE
UNIVERSITY PRESS

Credits

Illustration credits

Ralph Butler: 20, 29, 41, 54, 61; Mark Collins: 17, 30, 46, 56; Paul Daviz: 34, 58; Chuck Gonzales: 4, 13, 18, 62; Dan Hubig: 8 (*bottom*), 14, 16, 37, 57, 65; Kja-Artists.com: 5 (*top*), 25, 33, 45, 49; Trevor Keen: 38; Joanna Kerr: 8 (*top*), 26; Monika Melnychuk/i2iart.com: 6, 9, 28; Karen Minot: 50; Ortelius Design: 10, 12; Robert Schuster: 5 (*bottom*), 36, 47; Russ Willms: 48, 63; James Yamasaki: 2, 22, 53

Photography credits

10 (*left to right*) ©Best View Stock/Age Fotostock; ©Guy Needham/National Geographic My Shot/National Geographic Stock; ©Age Fotostock/SuperStock; 12 ©Leonid Plotkin/Alamy; 24 (*clockwise from top left*) ©Mood Board/Age Fotostock; ©Jin Akaishi/Aflo Foto Agency/Photolibrary; ©Jose Luis Pelaez Inc./Age Fotostock; ©Simon Willms/Lifesize/Getty Images; 36 (*left to right*) ©Bonchan/Shutterstock; ©iStockphoto/Thinkstock; ©Edie Layland/istockphoto; ©iStockphoto/Thinkstock; 40 (*center*) ©Ryan McVay/Stockbyte/Getty Images; (*clockwise from top left*) © Flirt/SuperStock; ©All Canada Photos/SuperStock; ©Aispix/Shutterstock; ©Al Bello/Staff/Getty Images Sport/Getty Images; ©Comstock/Getty Images; ©Jim Cummins/Taxi/Getty Images; ©Imagemore Co., Ltd./Getty Images; 42 (*top row, left to right*) ©Corbis/Photolibrary; ©Age Fotostock/SuperStock; ©Glowimages/Getty Images; ©Fstockfoto/Shutterstock; (*bottom row, left to right*) ©James Quine/Alamy; ©Lite Productions/Glow Images RF/Photolibrary; ©Gregory Dale/National Geographic Stock; ©Kord/Age Fotostock; 44 (*center*) © Ramon Purcell/Istockphoto; (*clockwise from top left*) ©Jim Loscalzo/EPA/Corbis; ©Alex Wong/Staff/Getty Images; ©The Washington Post/Contributor/Getty Images; ©Stock Connection/SuperStock; ©Jim Young/Reuters/Corbis; ©GlowImages/Age Fotostock; 58 (*left to right*) ©Andrew H. Walker/Getty Images; ©Walter McBride/Retna Ltd/Corbis; ©AP Photo/Julie Jacobson; ©Disney/Joan Marcus/Photofest; ©AP Photo/Stuart Ramson; ©Bruce Glikas/FilmMagic/Getty Images; 59 ©Zoonar/Paul Hakimata/Age Fotostock

Plan of Intro Video A

1 Welcome!

1 VOCABULARY *People and names*

PAIR WORK Fill in the blanks. Use the words in the box. Then compare with a partner.

> ✓ first   friends   last   student   teacher

1. Hi. My ....first.... name is Caroline. My .... call me Carol.

2. Ms. Lee is my .... I'm her .... My name's Alex Sims.

3. Hello. I'm Eduardo. My .... name is Robles.

2 INTRODUCTIONS

A Check (✓) the correct responses. Then compare with a partner.

1. Hello.
   - ☐ Excuse me.
   - ✓ Hi.

2. My name is Molly. What's your name?
   - ☐ I'm Peter.
   - ☐ My friends call me Molly.

3. Hi, Pete. It's nice to meet you.
   - ☐ Nice to meet you, too.
   - ☐ Yes, I am.

4. Hello. I'm Peter Krum.
   - ☐ Hello. What's your name?
   - ☐ Hi, Peter. Nice to meet you.

B **PAIR WORK** Practice the conversations in part A. Use your own names.

3 WHAT DO YOU SEE?

Watch the first 30 seconds of the video with the sound off. Check (✓) the correct answers.

1. Peter is
   - ☐ a student.
   - ☐ a teacher.

2. Molly is
   - ☐ a student.
   - ☐ a teacher.

4 GET THE PICTURE

A Check your answers to Exercise 3.
Are they correct?

B Match. Then compare with a partner.

1. ....*c*.... Molly
2. .... Peter
3. .... Mrs. Smith
4. .... Miss Taylor

C Match the first names or titles with the last names. Then compare with a partner.

A	B
1. Miss	a. Krum
2. Mrs.	b. Lin
3. Peter	c. Smith
4. Molly	d. Taylor

5 WATCH FOR DETAILS

Check (✓) the correct answers. Then compare with a partner.

1. Peter's nickname is
   ☐ Krum.
   ☑ Pete.

2. Molly's friends call her
   ☐ Molly.
   ☐ Holly.

3. Peter is Molly's
   ☐ friend.
   ☐ classmate.

4. Molly and Peter's class is at
   ☐ 8:00.
   ☐ 9:00.

5. Mrs. Smith
   ☐ is Molly and Peter's teacher.
   ☐ is not Molly and Peter's teacher.

6. Miss Taylor's class is in Room
   ☐ 201.
   ☐ 203.

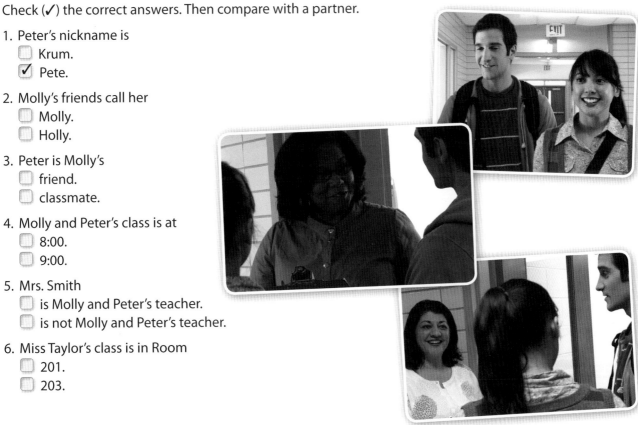

6 DO YOU REMEMBER?

Write the sentences under the correct picture. Then compare with a partner.

He's Molly's classmate.
Her last name is Taylor.
Her room is 201.
✓ She's not a teacher.

She's Peter's teacher.
She's the teacher in Room 203.
His teacher is Miss Taylor.
She's not Molly's teacher.

His class is not in Room 201.
Her last name is Smith.
She's Peter's classmate.
Her teacher is Miss Taylor.

She's not a teacher.

....
....
....

Follow-up

7 NICE TO MEET YOU

A Match.

A
1. It's nice to meet you, Sarah.
2. Hello. I'm Paul Thompson.
3. Are you a student here?

B
a. Yes, I am.
b. Nice to meet you, too.
c. Hi. My name is Sarah Long.

B **PAIR WORK** Put the sentences in order. Then practice the conversation.

A: Hello. I'm Paul Thompson.

B: Hi. My name is Sarah Long.

A: ....

B: ....

A: ....

B: ....

C **CLASS ACTIVITY** Now introduce yourself around the class. Use your own information.

Interchange Intro VRB © Cambridge University Press 2012 Photocopiable

☰ Language close-up

8 WHAT DID THEY SAY?

Watch the video and complete the conversation. Then practice it.

Molly and Peter are at school.

Molly: Excuse me. Um, ...hello............. .
Peter: .... !
Molly: .... name is Molly.
      What's .... name?
Peter: .... Peter. My .... call me Pete.
Molly: My friends .... me . . . Molly.
      Hi, Pete. It's nice to .... you.
Peter: It's nice to meet you, ...
Molly: Are you a .... here?
Peter: .... , I am. My .... is at
      nine o'clock with .... Taylor.
Molly: Miss Taylor? .... my teacher. You're in
      .... class.
Peter: .... !

9 THE VERB BE *Asking for and giving information*

A Complete the conversations with the correct forms of *be*.
Then practice with a partner.

1. A: Excuse me. ....Are....... you Sam?
   B: No, I .... Luis. Sam .... over there.

2. A: I .... Celia. What .... your name?
   B: My name .... Dan.

3. A: .... this Mrs. Costa's classroom?
   B: No. Her class .... in Room 105.

4. A: What .... your email address?
   B: It .... marymary@email.com.

5. A: What .... your phone number?
   B: It .... (646) 555-7841.

B PAIR WORK Practice the conversations again.
Use your own information.

C GROUP WORK Now ask five students from
your class for their contact information.

A: What's your phone number, David?
B: It's (201) 555-3192.
A: 555-3182?
B: No, 3192.
A: OK, thanks.

David Chang
(201) 555-3192
@ dchang@email.com

2 My passport!

1 VOCABULARY *Prepositions*

A Look at the pictures. Where are these things? Circle the correct locations.

the wallet

1

in / on
the table

the keys

2

under / behind
the sofa

the umbrella

3

next to / under
the door

the cell phone

4

in / on
the TV

the passport

5

in front of / behind
the bag

the camera

6

in front of / behind
the books

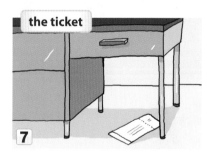

the ticket

7

on / under
the desk

the notebooks

8

in front of / in
the drawer

the books

9

next to / on
the table

B **PAIR WORK** Ask and answer questions about the things in part A.

A: Where is the wallet?   A: Where are the keys?
B: It's on the table.   B: They're . . .

2 WHAT DO YOU SEE?

Watch the video with the sound off. Check (✓) **True** or **False**. Correct the false sentences. Then compare with a partner.

	True	False
1. The ticket is ~~under~~ ᵒⁿ the TV.	☐	✓
2. The camera is in a box next to the sofa.	☐	☐
3. The keys are on the TV.	☐	☐
4. The passport is behind the desk.	☐	☐

☰ Watch the video

3 GET THE PICTURE

What things do Sofia and Jessica find? Number the things from 1 to 7 in the order they are found. Then compare with a partner.

.... her bag   .... her ticket

.... her camera   .... her umbrella

.... her keys   ....1.... her wallet

.... her passport

4 WATCH FOR DETAILS

Check (✓) the correct answers. Then compare with a partner.

1. At the beginning of the story, it's
   ☐ nine o'clock.
   ✓ ten o'clock.

2. Sofia's flight is at
   ☐ twelve-thirty.
   ☐ two-thirty.

3. Sofia's trip is to
   ☐ Peru.
   ☐ Brazil.

4. Sofia's desk is in the
   ☐ bedroom.
   ☐ living room.

5. Sofia is on a plane to
   ☐ Brazil.
   ☐ Budapest.

5 WHERE IS IT?

A Where are these things in the video? Fill in the blanks. Then compare with a partner.

1. The pen is ....*on*........ the TV.

2. The magazines are .... the coffee table.

3. The lamp is .... the TV.

4. The coffee table is .... the sofa.

B Where are Sofia's things? Complete the sentences. Then compare with a partner.

1. Sofia's wallet is *in her bag*.................................... .
2. Her ticket is on the TV, ...
3. Her camera is ....
4. Her keys are ....
5. Her passport is ....
6. Her bag is ....
7. Her umbrella is ....

☰ Follow-up

6 TRUE OR FALSE?

PAIR WORK Your partner puts some of your things in different places. Can you guess where?

A: My keys are in the desk.
B: True.

A: My ruler is on the desk.
B: False. It's under the desk.

Language close-up

7 *WHAT DID THEY SAY?*

Watch the video and complete the conversation. Then practice it.

Sofia is looking for her things.

Jessica: Sofia! Where's your ......*passport*...... ?

Sofia: .... it's . . . maybe it's .... a box!

Jessica: Oh!

Sofia: Maybe it's. . . . It's probably .... the chair.

Jessica: No, ... not here.

Sofia: OK. Maybe it's .... to the ....

Jessica: Sofia! .... this?

Sofia: My .... I'm going to need that. . . .
My .... !

Jessica: Is it .... the books? No.

Sofia: Oh, no!

Jessica: Sofia, are those .... keys, in .... of the TV?

Sofia: Yes, those are .... keys. . . . My passport, Jessica!
Wait a minute. Wait a minute. It's on the .... in the bedroom!

8 *PREPOSITIONS OF PLACE* *Describing location*

A Complete the sentences about the things in the picture.
Use each preposition only once. Then compare with a partner.

behind	in	in front of	✓next to	on	under

1. The purse *is next to the sofa* ....
2. The notebooks ....
3. The wallet ....
4. The lamp ....
5. The sunglasses ....
6. The clock ....

B Write similar sentences about things in your classroom.
Then read your sentences to your partner.

1. ....
2. ....
3. ....
4. ....
5. ....
6. ....

Newcomers High School

Preview

1 VOCABULARY *Countries and regions*

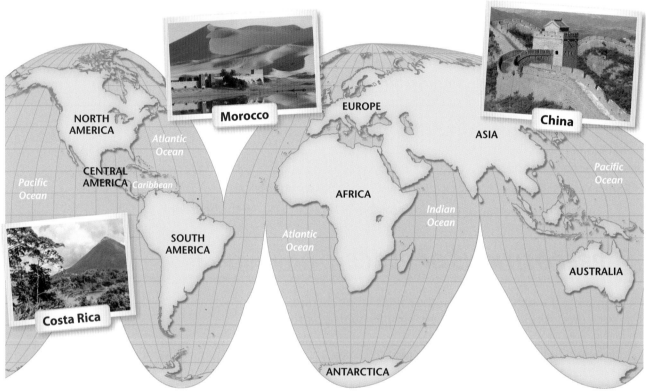

Countries		Regions
....b.... 1. China		a. Africa
.... 2. Costa Rica		b. Asia
.... 3. the Dominican Republic		c. Europe
.... 4. Italy		d. Central America
.... 5. Mexico		e. North America
.... 6. Morocco		f. South America
.... 7. Uruguay		g. the Caribbean
.... 8.		
.... 9.		

A Match. Then add two more countries to the list.

B **PAIR WORK** Ask and answer questions about the places in part A.

A: Where's China?
B: It's in Asia. **or**
   I think it's in . . . **or**
   I'm not sure. Is it in . . . ?

2 GUESS THE FACTS

Complete the chart. Use the words in the box.
Then compare with a partner.

Arabic	✓ Casablanca	San José
Cantonese	Hong Kong	Spanish

A: Casablanca is in Morocco.
B: Yes, that's right. **or**
   No, it's not. It's in . . .

B: They speak Spanish in Morocco.
A: No, they speak . . .

Country	City	Language
1. Morocco	Casablanca	....
2. Costa Rica	....	....
3. China	....	....

☰ Watch the video

3 GET THE PICTURE

A Check your answers to Exercise 2.

B Where are they from?
Check (✓) the correct answers.

	Fatima	**Camilia**	**Cai**
China	☐	☐	☐
Costa Rica	☐	☐	☐
Morocco	✓	☐	☐

4 WATCH FOR DETAILS

Check (✓) the correct answers. Then compare with a partner.

1. Newcomers High School is in
   ☐ Washington, D.C.
   ✓ New York City.

2. The students at Newcomers High School
   ☐ are from the U.S.
   ☐ aren't from the U.S.

3. Morocco is on the
   ☐ ocean.
   ☐ river.

4. Camilia says the rain forest is
   ☐ fun.
   ☐ large.

5. Cai's brother is
   ☐ 20.
   ☐ 22.

6. Cai's brother is
   ☐ talkative.
   ☐ serious.

7. Fatima speaks
   ☐ two languages.
   ☐ three languages.

8. *Ma'a salama* means
   ☐ "Thank you."
   ☐ "Good-bye."

5 WHERE IS IT?

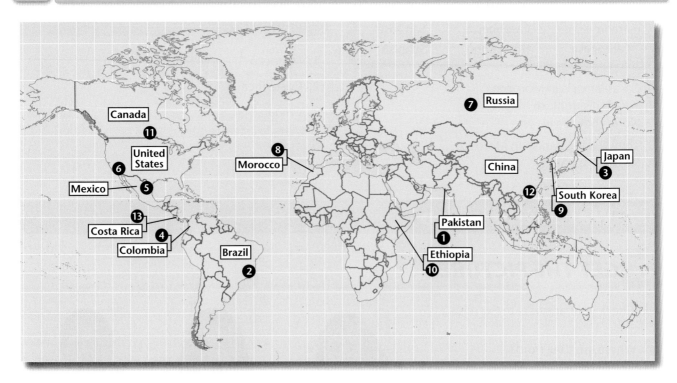

A **PAIR WORK** Students from Newcomers High School come from these cities. Find the cities on the map.

Casablanca	Hong Kong	San José

A: Where's Casablanca?
B: I think it's here, in . . . It's number . . .
A: You're right. **or** No. It's number . . . It's here, in . . .

B **PAIR WORK** Now take turns finding these cities.

Addis Ababa	Inchon	Monterrey	Sapporo	Winnipeg
Cali	Karachi	San Diego	St. Petersburg	Vitória

A: Where's Cali?
B: I think it's in Colombia. It's number 4.
A: Yes, that's right. **or** No, it's not. It's here, number . . .

C **GROUP WORK** Write five cities on five pieces of paper. Mix them up. Pick a city. Where is it?

A: Where's . . . ?
B: I think it's in . . .
A: That's right. **or** No, it's in . . .

Cali, Colombia

WHAT DID THEY SAY?

Watch the video and complete the conversation. Then practice it.

Rachel Park is talking to Camilia, a student at Newcomers High School.

Rachel: ....Hello........ . Where .... you from, Camilia?
Are .... from Morocco, too?

Camilia: No, I'm .... from Costa Rica.

Rachel: .... is Costa Rica, Camilia?

Camilia: .... in Central America.
I'm .... San José, the ....

Rachel: What's San José .... ?

Camilia: It's very .... I like it a lot.

Rachel: What are .... ?

Camilia: These .... photos of the rain forest in my ....
The rain forest is .... and interesting. It's fun, ...

Rachel: It looks fun! .... you, Camilia.

 PRESENT TENSE OF BE *Countries and regions*

A Complete the conversations. Then practice them.

1. A: How ....are........ you today?
   B: I .... fine, thank you.
   A: Where .... you from, Carlos?
   B: I .... from Mexico. How about you?
   A: I .... from Canada.
   B: Oh, ... you from Montreal?
   A: Yes, I ....

2. A: Where .... Rachel from?
   B: She .... from the U.S.
   A: .... she from New York?
   B: No, she .... not from New York.
   She .... from Chicago originally.

3. A: Where .... Ji-son and Hyo from?
   B: Ji-son .... from Pusan, and
   Hyo .... from Seoul.
   A: Oh, so they .... both from South Korea.
   B: Yes, they ....

Where are you from, Ji-son?

I'm from Pusan. How about you?

I'm from Seoul.

B CLASS ACTIVITY Now find out what cities (or countries) your classmates are from.

4 What are you wearing?

1 VOCABULARY *Clothing*

A Find these things in the picture. Match.

1. __d__ a dark blue suit	5. .... white socks	9. .... a backpack	13. .... a scarf
2. .... a brown tie	6. .... a gray skirt	10. .... boots	14. .... a yellow dress
3. .... black shoes	7. .... a white blouse	11. .... jeans	15. .... a pink hat
4. .... a briefcase	8. .... a blue jacket	12. .... a sweater	16. .... a red shirt

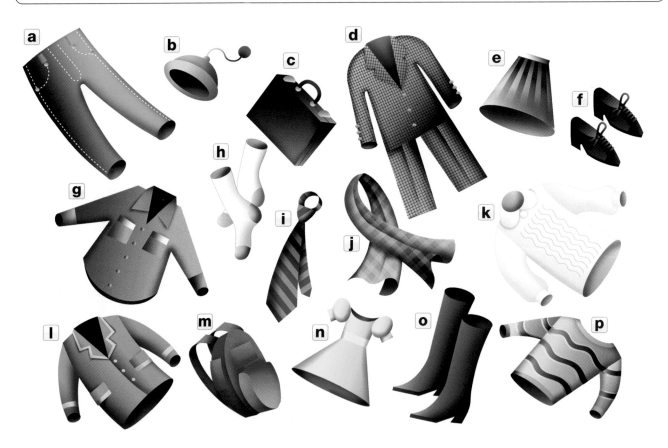

B **PAIR WORK** Cover the words in part A. Then ask about things in the picture.

A: What's this?
B: It's a dark blue suit.
A: What are these?
B: They're black shoes.

2 WHAT DO YOU SEE?

Watch the video with the sound off. Answer the questions.
Check (✓) all correct answers.

1. What is the man wearing and carrying?
   - ☐ a blue suit
   - ✓ a brown tie
   - ☐ brown shoes
   - ✓ a black briefcase

2. What is the uniform for the girl's school?
   - ☐ white socks
   - ☐ a red skirt
   - ☐ a white blouse
   - ☐ a green sweater

3. What are the mother and baby wearing?
   - ☐ sneakers
   - ☐ jeans
   - ☐ a T-shirt
   - ☐ a scarf
   - ☐ yellow pants
   - ☐ a pink hat

4. What is Jamal wearing today?
   - ☐ black pants
   - ☐ a green shirt
   - ☐ a coat

Watch the video

3 GET THE PICTURE

Check your answers to Exercise 2. Then compare with a partner.

4 WATCH FOR DETAILS

Watch the video again. This time, cross out the wrong items in Exercise 2. Write the correct ones. Then compare with a partner.

- ☐ a~~ blue suit~~ *a gray striped suit*
- ✓ a brown tie
- ☐ ~~brown shoes~~ *black shoes*
- ✓ a black briefcase

5 DO YOU REMEMBER?

Check (✓) the correct answers. Then compare with a partner.

1. The season is
   - ☐ spring.
   - ☐ fall.

2. The weather is cool and
   - ☐ cloudy.
   - ☐ sunny.

3. Megan's backpack is yellow, and Jasmin's backpack is
   - ☐ blue.
   - ☐ black.

4. Sheila and Julie are wearing
   - ☐ casual clothes.
   - ☐ formal clothes.

☰ Follow-up

6 WHAT'S YOUR OPINION?

A Do you like these people's clothes? Check (✓) your answers.

1. ☐ yes ☐ no

2. ☐ yes ☐ no

3. ☐ yes ☐ no

4. ☐ yes ☐ no

5. ☐ yes ☐ no

6. ☐ yes ☐ no

B PAIR WORK Compare your answers to part A.

A: I like his clothes. I like his gray suit.
B: I like his gray suit, and I like his brown tie.

> The negative of *like* is *don't like*.

"I like his gray suit, but I don't like his red tie."

7 WHAT DID THEY SAY?

Watch the video and complete the conversations.

Jamal Greene is asking people about their clothes.

1. Jamal: Excuse me. Hello!
   Man: ....Hello........ there.
   Jamal: .... talking to people about ....
       What are you .... today?
   Man: I'm wearing a .... striped suit,
       brown .... , and black ....
   Jamal: Is it a .... suit?
   Man: .... , it's for cool ....
       It's good for the fall and ....
   Jamal: Very .... , very formal.
   Man: Yes, I'm .... today, so I'm wearing
       formal ....
   Jamal: I ....

2. Jamal: So .... are you wearing .... ?
   Sheila: We're just wearing .... clothes.
       I have on boots and jeans, a .... ,
       a light jacket, and .... sunglasses.
   Jamal: And a very pretty .... scarf.
   Sheila: Thank you.
   Jamal: And what is Julie .... ?
   Sheila: She's wearing blue .... , a white .... ,
       a pink hat. It's her .... hat.

8 PRESENT CONTINUOUS *Asking about and describing clothing*

A Complete these conversations with the present continuous of *wear*.

1. A: ......Are...... you ...wearing... pants today?
   B: No, I .... a skirt.

2. A: What .... our teacher .... today?
   B: She .... a black sweater, a blue blouse, and a gray skirt.

3. A: What color shoes .... you .... ?
   B: I .... white shoes today.

4. A: .... your classmates .... coats today?
   B: No, they .... coats, but they .... sweaters.

5. A: What colors .... you .... today?
   B: I .... yellow, blue, brown, and green.

B **PAIR WORK** Practice the conversations again.
Use your own information.

Everybody's having fun.

1 VOCABULARY Actions

A Write the actions under the pictures. Then compare with a partner.

answering the phone	looking up a phone number	sleeping
babysitting	making popcorn	✓ studying
having dinner together	ordering a pizza	watching movies

Mimi

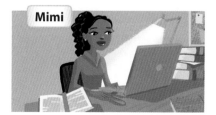

1. studying

Blake and Sam

2. ....

Dave

3. ....

Young-soo

4. ....

Jenny

5. ....

Jess and Kim

6. ....

Ken

7. ....

Amy

8. ....

the Sotos

9. ....

B **PAIR WORK** Ask and answer questions about the people in part A.

A: What's Mimi doing?
B: She's studying.
A: What are Blake and Sam doing?
B: They're . . .

2 WHAT DO YOU SEE?

Watch the video with the sound off. Put the pictures in order from 1 to 7.

.... Peter is studying. ....

....

Watch the video

3 GET THE PICTURE

A Check your answers to Exercise 2.

B Now write the correct description under each picture in Exercise 2. Use the ideas in the box. Then compare with a partner.

Peter / Kate / Doug / Emi is . . .
answering the phone.   sleeping.
babysitting.   ✓ studying.
calling a friend.   watching movies.
going out.

Peter

Kate

Doug

Emi

Check (✓) the correct answers. Then compare with a partner.

1. At the beginning of the video, it's
   ☐ 6:00.
   ✓ 7:00.

2. Peter is studying
   ☐ at home.
   ☐ in school.

3. Kate thinks babysitting
   ☐ is fun.
   ☐ isn't fun.

4. Peter calls Doug at
   ☐ 8:25.
   ☐ 7:25.

5. Doug is having dinner
   ☐ with his grandparents.
   ☐ at his girlfriend's house.

6. Emi calls Peter at
   ☐ 9:20.
   ☐ 8:20.

7. Emi, Ivan, and Carla are at
   ☐ Carla's place.
   ☐ Emi's place.

8. Emi, Ivan, and Carla are making
   ☐ a pizza.
   ☐ popcorn.

Follow-up

 5 *WHAT AM I DOING?*

PAIR WORK Take turns acting out an action and guessing the action.
Use the verbs in the box or your own ideas.

cook	drive	get up	read	shop	study
dance	eat	play	run	sleep	swim

A: What am I doing?
B: Are you dancing?
A: No, I'm not.
B: Are you swimming?
A: Yes, I am.

6 WHAT DID THEY SAY?

Watch the video and complete the conversation. Then practice it.

Emi is calling Peter.

Peter: Uh, ...hello.......... ?

Emi: Hi, Peter. .... Emi.
Um, ... you OK?

Peter: I'm ....

Emi: .... not studying. You're .... !

Peter: OK, OK. I'm .... But I'm .... ,
too! .... are you doing, Emi?

Emi: I'm hanging out .... Ivan
and Carla.

Peter: .... ? Sounds like fun.

Emi: Yeah. We're .... movies at my place.
.... you busy?

Peter: Well, I'm studying for a test that I have
on ....

Emi: We're .... popcorn.

Peter: What .... is it?

Emi: It's .... after nine. Ivan is .... a pizza.

Peter: OK! I'm ....

7 PRESENT CONTINUOUS *Describing current activities*

A Complete these conversations. Use the correct present continuous
forms of the verbs in parentheses. Then practice with a partner.

1. A: What 's Pablo ......doing........ (do)?
   B: He .... (study).

2. A: What .... Mariko .... (read)?
   B: She .... (read) a really good book.

3. A: What .... your family .... (do) right now?
   B: My parents .... (work), and my brother and sister
   .... (talk) on the phone.

4. A: What .... our teacher .... (do)?
   B: He .... (have) lunch.
   A: Really? I .... (get) hungry, too.

5. A: .... you .... (speak) Spanish right now?
   B: No, I .... (speak) English!

B **PAIR WORK** Now ask and answer similar questions about your classmates,
friends, and family. Use your own information.

My life

1 VOCABULARY Daily routines

Look at Vanessa's daily routine. Write the sentences under the pictures.
Then compare with a partner.

> I walk to work.   Every night, I write jokes.
> ✓ Weekdays, I get up at 7:30.   I have breakfast with my parents.
> At 5:00, I finish work.   I start work at 9:00.
> At 1:30, I take a lunch break.   On Saturdays, I tell my jokes at a comedy club.

1. Weekdays, I get up at 7:30.

2. ....

3. ....

4. ....

5. ....

6. ....

7. ....

8. ....

GUESS THE FACTS

Look again at the sentences in Exercise 1. Where do you think Vanessa works? Check (✓) your answer.

☐ She works at a school.   ☐ She works in an office.   ☐ She works at home.

3 WHAT DO YOU SEE?

Watch the first minute of the video with the sound off. Check your answer to Exercise 2.

Watch the video

4 GET THE PICTURE

A Complete the description.

On weekdays, Vanessa ⎯⎯*designs web pages*⎯⎯ all day,
and she ⎯⎯⎯⎯⎯⎯⎯⎯⎯⎯⎯ at night.

B Check (✓) **True** or **False**. Then compare with a partner.

	True	False
1. Vanessa lives with her brother.	☐	✓
2. Vanessa's mother is a teacher.	☐	☐
3. Vanessa's father walks to work.	☐	☐
4. In the evening, Vanessa writes stories.	☐	☐
5. On Saturdays, Vanessa goes to a comedy club.	☐	☐
6. Vanessa gets home early from the club.	☐	☐
7. On Sundays, Vanessa works all day.	☐	☐

5 WATCH FOR DETAILS

Check (✓) the correct answers. Then compare with a partner.

1. How old is Vanessa?
   ☐ 25
   ✓ 22

2. What is Vanessa's brother's name?
   ☐ Wynton
   ☐ William

3. What time does Vanessa's mother take the bus?
   ☐ 8:30 A.M.
   ☐ 9:00 A.M.

4. What time does Vanessa's father start work?
   ☐ 9:00 A.M.
   ☐ 9:30 P.M.

5. What time does the show at the club start?
   ☐ 8:00 P.M.
   ☐ 9:00 P.M.

6. When does Vanessa usually go home from the club?
   ☐ Around 11:00 P.M.
   ☐ Around 12:00 A.M.

VIDEO ACTIVITIES

Interchange Intro VRB © Cambridge University Press 2012   Photocopiable   *Unit 6* ▪ **23**

DO YOU REMEMBER?

PAIR WORK Complete the chart. Check (✓) the words that describe Vanessa's routine.

	On weekdays	At night	On weekends
Designs web pages	☐	☐	☐
Writes jokes	☐	☐	☐
Tells jokes	☐	☐	☐
Goes downtown	☐	☐	☐

☰ Follow-up

7 A DAY IN THE LIFE

A **PAIR WORK** Choose one of these people. Describe a day in the person's life. Use the ideas in the box below or your own ideas. Your partner guesses the person.

A: He gets up at 1:00 in the afternoon. He starts work at 10:00 at night.
B: I think he's a musician.

a musician

a reporter

a teacher

a waiter

He/She . . .
gets up at 5:00 in the morning.
gets up at 1:00 in the afternoon.
finishes work at 3:00 in the morning.
has breakfast at work.
starts work at 10:00 at night.
wears a white shirt and black pants at work.
finishes work at 3:00 in the afternoon.
works for a television station.
doesn't work on weekends.
sometimes has lunch with students.
writes on the board.

B **GROUP WORK** Now share your descriptions with another pair. Your partners guess who you're describing.

8 WHAT DID SHE SAY?

Watch the video and complete the descriptions. Then practice it.

Vanessa is talking about her life.

Hi, I'm Vanessa. Welcome to my ....home................ . I live ....
Come on in! This is my .... , and this is my ....
This is my .... , Wynton. He doesn't ....
with us. He has his own .... He's ....
I'm 22, so that makes him .... big brother.

.... , I get up around 7:30. We ....
breakfast at about eight .... , right here. My mom is
a teacher. She .... in the school. She takes the
.... to work. The bus comes at .... , and she gets
home about .... My dad .... to work. He works
.... the clinic. .... a doctor. He starts work at
.... o'clock and gets home at ....

9 SIMPLE PRESENT TENSE *Talking about routines*

A Complete these conversations with the correct verb forms.
Then practice the conversations.

1. A: ....Do........ (Do/Does) you live in the city?
   B: No, I .... (don't/doesn't). I .... (live/lives)
      in the suburbs. My sister .... (live/lives) in the city.
      She .... (have/has) a good job there.

2. A: How .... (do/does) you go to school?
   B: I .... (take/takes) the bus because
      I .... (don't/doesn't) have a car.

3. A: What time .... (do/does) you go to school?
   B: Well, the bus .... (come/comes) at 7:00.

4. A: .... (Do/Does) you have breakfast every day?
   B: Yes, I .... (do/does). My parents ....
      (don't/doesn't) work in the morning, but they ....
      (get up/gets up) early and .... (have/has) breakfast with
      me. Then my father .... (drive/drives) me to the bus.

5. A: Where .... (do/does) you have dinner?
   B: My friends and I .... (go/goes) to a restaurant after class,
      so I .... (don't/doesn't) have dinner with my family.

B **PAIR WORK** Ask and answer the questions again. Use your
own information.

Richdale Street

1 VOCABULARY *A new apartment*

A Find these places in the picture.
Match. Then compare with a partner.

1. ....*f*.... bathroom
2. .... bedroom
3. .... closet
4. .... kitchen
5. .... living room
6. .... yard

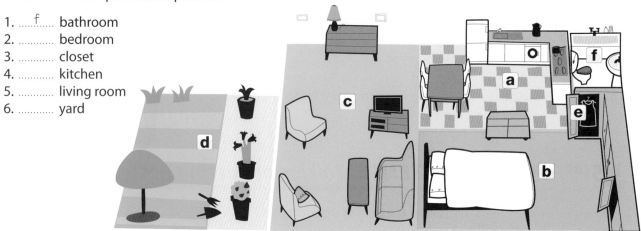

B **PAIR WORK** What do you need in a new apartment? Number
the things from 1 (most important) to 10 (least important).

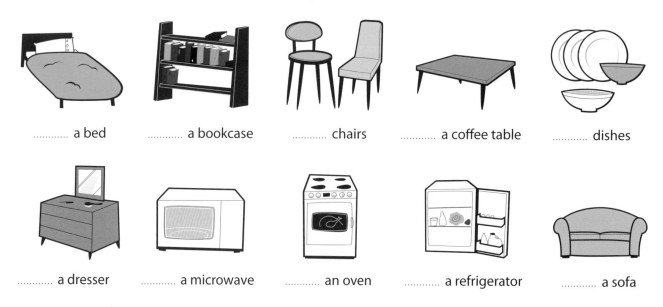

.... a bed   .... a bookcase   .... chairs   .... a coffee table   .... dishes

.... a dresser   .... a microwave   .... an oven   .... a refrigerator   .... a sofa

C **GROUP WORK** Now compare your answers. Use your own ideas, too.

A: I think you need a refrigerator for the kitchen.
B: And you also need a sofa for the living room.
C: Well, I think you need . . .

2 WHAT DO YOU SEE?

Watch the video with the sound off. What things do the two roommates have? Check (✓) them. Then compare with a partner.

- ☑ a sofa
- ☐ shelves
- ☐ a refrigerator
- ☐ a dresser
- ☐ a coffee table
- ☐ a microwave
- ☐ dishes
- ☐ a bed
- ☐ chairs
- ☐ a stove
- ☐ a coffeemaker
- ☐ a television

≡ Watch the video

3 GET THE PICTURE

Jessica tells her mother about her apartment. What information is true, and what information is false? Check (✓) the correct answers. Then compare with a partner.

	True	False
1. Sofia waves hello to Jessica's mom.	☑	☐
2. There's no microwave.	☐	☐
3. The kitchen is very sunny.	☐	☐
4. There's a modern refrigerator.	☐	☐
5. The kitchen is clean.	☐	☐
6. The bedroom has a lot of windows.	☐	☐
7. The bedroom has a great view.	☐	☐
8. There's a closet in the bedroom.	☐	☐
9. They don't have a yard.	☐	☐
10. The vase is in the living room.	☐	☐

4 WATCH FOR DETAILS

Check (✓) the correct answers. Then compare with a partner.

1. Who is on the phone?
   - ☑ Jessica's mother.
   - ☐ Sofia's mother.

2. What's the view from Jessica's bedroom?
   - ☐ A park.
   - ☐ A wall.

3. What's the present from Jessica's mother?
   - ☐ A lamp.
   - ☐ A vase.

4. What's Jessica and Sofia's address?
   - ☐ 238 Richdale Street.
   - ☐ 283 Richdale Street.

5. Where is Jessica's mother calling from?
   - ☐ The suburbs.
   - ☐ The city.

6. What does Jessica's mother say about the apartment?
   - ☐ She says it's nice.
   - ☐ She says it's perfect.

WHAT'S YOUR OPINION?

What important things do you think Jessica and Sofia still need? Check (✓) them.
Then compare with a partner.

☑ an armchair   ☑ a rug   ☑ curtains

☑ a microwave   ☑ a dining table   ☑ pictures

A: I think they need . . .
B: But they don't really need . . .

☰ Follow-up

6 ROLE PLAY

A What questions do you think Jessica's mother asks about the new apartment?
Write six more questions.

1. Do you like your new apartment?
2. How many rooms are there?
3. ....
4. ....
5. ....
6. ....
7. ....
8. ....

> We have an oven, but we don't have a microwave.

B **GROUP WORK** Now ask and answer questions.
Two people play the roles of Jessica and Sofia.

A: Do you like your new apartment?
B: Yes, we do.
A: How many rooms are there?
C: There are four rooms.

☰ Language close-up

7 WHAT DID SHE SAY?

Watch the video and complete the conversation. Then practice it.

Jessica is talking to her mother on the phone and answering her questions.

Jessica: She's asking about our apartment. . . . Yeah, I ....*like*........... it.

Well, let me see. There are .... rooms: the living
room, the .... , and two bedrooms. Oh, and of
course, a ....

The .... room? Well, it's really big. The kitchen
is .... , too.

No, we don't have a .... We just ....
a regular oven.

Yes, the kitchen is very .... There is a
modern ....

Clean? Yeah, of course, ... clean.

The bedroom? Actually, there are a .... of big
windows. And the .... is really ....

8 THERE IS/THERE ARE *Describing a home*

A Complete these sentences with **there's**, **there are**, and **there aren't**.

1. ......*There are*...... eight rooms in our house,
   and .... a garage, too.
2. .... some trees in the yard,
   but .... any flowers.
3. .... some armchairs in the living room,
   and .... a large table in the dining room.
4. .... any pictures in the dining room,
   but .... some in the living room.
5. .... a stove and a refrigerator in the kitchen,
   but .... no microwave oven.
6. .... three bedrooms in the house,
   and .... one bathroom.

B Rewrite the sentences in part A so that they are true for
your house or apartment. Then compare with a partner.

The night shift

1 VOCABULARY Jobs

A Write the jobs under the pictures. Then compare with a partner.

| ambulance driver | ✓ doctor | taxi driver | waiter |

1. _doctor_

2. ....

3. ....

4. ....

B PAIR WORK Choose a job from part A. Say what you do. Use the sentences in the box or your own ideas. Your partner guesses the job.

I take people to the emergency room.	I wear a uniform.
I work at night.	I help sick people.
I sit all day / all night.	I stand all day / all night.
I work in a hospital.	I work in a restaurant.

A: I stand all day.
B: Are you a doctor?
A: No, I'm a waiter.

2 WHAT DO YOU SEE?

Watch the video with the sound off. Write each person's job. Then compare with a partner.

1. .... 2. ....

3. .... 4. ....

☰ Watch the video

3 GET THE PICTURE

A Check your answers to Exercise 2. Were they correct?

B These people work at night. What time do they start? What time do they finish?
Write the times. Then compare with a partner.

	Eva	Trey	Dwayne	Gio
Starts	11:00 p.m.			
Finishes				

4 WATCH FOR DETAILS

Check (✓) the correct answers. Then compare with a partner.

Eva

1. Eva North thinks her job is ....
   - ☐ dangerous
   - ☑ stressful

2. Eva .... her job.
   - ☐ likes
   - ☐ doesn't like

Dwayne

5. Dwayne goes to school in the ....
   - ☐ morning
   - ☐ afternoon

6. Dwayne wakes up about ....
   - ☐ 10:00 P.M.
   - ☐ 12:00 P.M.

7. .... is a hard day for Dwayne.
   - ☐ Tuesday
   - ☐ Thursday

Trey

3. Trey thinks his job is ....
   - ☐ busy, but interesting
   - ☐ difficult, but exciting

4. Trey works for .... hours, and then he has a breakfast break.
   - ☐ five
   - ☐ seven

Gio

8. Taxi drivers on the night shift often work .... hours.
   - ☐ 10 to 15
   - ☐ 12 to 14

9. It's .... when Rachel speaks to Gio.
   - ☐ 6:00 A.M.
   - ☐ 7:00 A.M.

10. Gio thinks he .... hard.
    - ☐ works
    - ☐ doesn't work

☰ Follow-up

5 ROLE PLAY

 Play the roles of the people in the video. Give your real opinion of the jobs. Use the words in the box.

dangerous	easy	interesting	relaxing	stressful
difficult	exciting	pleasant	safe	unpleasant

A: What do you do, Eva?
B: I'm a doctor.
A: Oh, that's an exciting job!
B: Yes, but it's very stressful.

                    Interchange Intro VRB © Cambridge University Press 2012   Photocopiable

Language close-up

VIDEO ACTIVITIES

6 WHAT DID THEY SAY?

Watch the video and complete the conversation. Then practice it.

A reporter is talking to people who work at night.

Rachel: I'm Rachel Park, and I'm ......standing...... in front of
Memorial Hospital with Eva North. She works
.... in the hospital. Eva, ...
do you do?

Eva: I'm a ....

Rachel: .... do you work, exactly?

Eva: Right here in the emergency ....

Rachel: Is it .... at night?

Eva: Yes, yes, it ....

Rachel: Really?

Eva: All .... and all night.

Rachel: .... do you like your job?

Eva: It's .... I work .... hours – from
11:00 to 7:00. But .... day
in the hospital is different. I .... it. . . . Oh,
actually, I'm .... I have to go.

7 SIMPLE PRESENT TENSE *Talking about work and school*

A Complete these conversations. Use the correct forms of the verb. Then practice the conversations.

1. A: ......Does..... Dwayne .....work...... (work) at night?

   B: Yes, he .... (do). He .... (go) to school in the morning
   and .... (do) his homework in the afternoon.

   A: When .... he .... (sleep)?

   B: That's a good question!

2. A: Where .... Eva and Trey .... (work)?

   B: They .... (work) at a hospital.

   A: What .... they .... (do), exactly?

   B: Eva .... (take) care of sick people, and Trey
   .... (drive) an ambulance.

B **PAIR WORK** Now ask your partner these questions.

1. Do you have classes during the day? What time do you go to school?
2. How do you go to school? How do you go home?
3. When do you do your homework? Where do you do it?
4. Do you have a job? Do you work at night?

Interchange Intro VRB © Cambridge University Press 2012   Photocopiable   *Unit 8 ▪ 33*

This page is intentionally left blank

interchange
FIFTH EDITION

intro A

Workbook

Jack C. Richards

Contents

Credits

The authors and publishers acknowledge the following sources of copyright material and are grateful for the permissions granted. While every effort has been made, it has not always been possible to identify the sources of all the material used, or to trace all copyright holders. If any omissions are brought to our notice, we will be happy to include the appropriate acknowledgements on reprinting and in the next update to the digital edition, as applicable.

Key: B = Below, BC = Below Centre, BL = Below Left, BR = Below Right, C = Centre, CL = Centre Left, CR = Centre Right, Ex = Exercise, L = Left, R = Right, T = Top, TC = Top Centre, TL = Top Left, TR = Top Right.

Illustrations

337 Jon (KJA Artists): 11, 21, 81; **417 Neal** (KJA Artists): 1, 58; **Mark Duffin**: 7, 12, 26, 37, 41, 52, 70; **Thomas Girard** (Good Illustration): 10, 63, 68, 84; **John Goodwin** (Eye Candy Illustration): 23, 71; **Dusan Lakicevic** (Beehive Illustration): 57; **Quino Marin** (The Organisation): 19, 69, 92, 94; **Gavin Reece** (New Division): 5, 39; **Gary Venn** (Lemonade Illustration): 25, 74, 77; **Paul Williams** (Sylvie Poggio Artists): 6, 29, 67.

Photos

Back cover (woman with whiteboard): Jenny Acheson/Stockbyte/GettyImages; Back cover (whiteboard): Nemida/GettyImages; Back cover (man using phone): Betsie Van Der Meer/Taxi/GettyImages; Back cover (woman smiling): PeopleImages.com/DigitalVision/GettyImages; Back cover (name tag): Tetra Images/GettyImages; Back cover (handshake): David Lees/Taxi/GettyImages; p. 2 (TL): Yellow Dog Productions/Iconica/GettyImages; p. 2 (CR): Morsa Images/DigitalVision/GettyImages; p. 2 (BL): Johnny Greig/iStock/Getty Images Plus/GettyImages; p. 3: Nicolas McComber/E+/GettyImages; p. 4: MichaelDeLeon/iStock/Getty Images Plus/GettyImages; p. 5: Steve Debenport/E+/GettyImages; p. 8 (TL): hudiemm/E+/GettyImages; p. 8 (TC): Marek Mnich/E+/GettyImages; p. 8 (TR): Dorling Kindersley/Dorling Kindersley/GettyImages; p. 8 (CL): Tpopova/iStock/Getty Images Plus/GettyImages; p. 8 (C): Tpopova/iStock/Getty Images Plus/GettyImages; p. 8 (CR): Creative Crop/DigitalVision/GettyImages; p. 8 (BR): Betsie Van Der Meer/Taxi/GettyImages; p. 9 (TR): michaeljung/iStock/Getty Images Plus/GettyImages; p. 9 (B): Milk & Honey Creative/Stockbyte/GettyImages; p. 13: Martin Barraud/OJO Images/GettyImages; p. 14 (TL): Lumina Images/Blend Images/GettyImages; p. 14 (TR): Elyse Lewin/Photographer's Choice/GettyImages; p. 14 (BL): Fabrice LEROUGE/ONOKY/GettyImages; p. 14 (BR): Susan Chiang/iStock/Getty Images Plus/GettyImages; p. 15 (TL): franckreporter/E+/GettyImages; p. 15 (TR): AWL Images/AWL Images/GettyImages; p. 15 (CL): Image Source/Image Source/GettyImages; p. 15 (CR): Matthias Tunger/Photolibrary/GettyImages; p. 15 (BL): MATTES RenÃ©/hemis.fr/hemis.fr/GettyImages; p. 15 (BR): Luis Davilla/Photolibrary/GettyImages; p. 16: Bruce Glikas/FilmMagic/GettyImages; p. 17 (TL): Digital Vision/Digital Vision/GettyImages; p. 17 (CL): Thomas Barwick/Iconica/GettyImages; p. 17 (C): skynesher/E+/GettyImages; p. 17 (BC): Hans Neleman/The Image Bank/GettyImages; p. 17 (BL): RunPhoto/Photodisc/GettyImages; p. 17 (CR): Portra Images/Taxi/GettyImages; p. 17 (BR): Terry Vine/Blend Images/GettyImages; p. 18: Jupiterimages/Stockbyte/GettyImages; p. 20: Hero Images/Hero Images/GettyImages; p. 22 (TL): Gabriela Tulian/Moment/GettyImages; p. 22 (TR): James A. Guilliam/Photolibrary/GettyImages; p. 22 (CL): Stuart Stevenson photography/Moment/GettyImages; p. 22 (CR): Cultura RM Exclusive/Stephen Lux/Cultura Exclusive/GettyImages; p. 22 (BL): Robert Daly/Caiaimage/GettyImages; p. 22 (BR): noelbesuzzi/RooM/GettyImages; p. 24 (TL): Tim Robberts/Taxi/GettyImages; p. 24 (TR): Jan Scherders/Blend Images/GettyImages; p. 24 (BL): Chris Whitehead/Cultura/GettyImages; p. 24 (BR): A J James/Photodisc/GettyImages; p. 26: Paul Bradbury/Caiaimage/GettyImages; p. 27 (TL): Caiaimage/Trevor Adeline/Caiaimage/GettyImages; p. 27 (TC): Hero Images/Hero Images/GettyImages; p. 27 (TR): Westend61//GettyImages; p. 27 (CL): Susan Chiang/E+/GettyImages; p. 27 (C): shapecharge/E+/GettyImages; p. 27 (CR): Image Source/Image Source/GettyImages; p. 27 (BL): Henrik Sorensen/Iconica/GettyImages; p. 27 (BC): Hero Images/Hero Images/GettyImages; p. 27 (BR): Dougal Waters/DigitalVision/GettyImages; p. 28 (Ex 6.1): Hoxton/Tom Merton/Hoxton/GettyImages; p. 28 (Ex 6.2): Mike Harrington/The Image Bank/GettyImages; p. 28 (Ex 6.3): Alexander Rhind/Stone/GettyImages; p. 28 (Ex 6.4): Vico Collective/Alin Dragulin/Blend Images/GettyImages; p. 28 (Ex 6.5): Leonardo Patrizi/E+/GettyImages; p. 28 (Ex 6.6): JGI/Tom Grill/Blend Images/GettyImages; p. 28 (Ex 6.7): elenaleonova/iStock/Getty Images Plus/GettyImages; p. 28 (Ex 6.8): Thomas Barwick/Iconica/GettyImages; p. 30: Tetra Images/Tetra Images/GettyImages; p. 31 (TL): Caiaimage/Sam Edwards/Caiaimage/GettyImages; p. 31 (TR): Shestock/Blend Images/GettyImages; p. 31 (C): Marc Romanelli/Blend Images/GettyImages; p. 32: Dave & Les Jacobs/Blend Images/Getty Images Plus/GettyImages; p. 33: Dan Porges/Photolibrary/GettyImages; p. 33: Sam Edwards/Caiaimage/GettyImages; p. 34: Hero Images/Hero Images/GettyImages; p. 35: Hero Images/Hero Images/GettyImages; p. 36: XiXinXing/XiXinXing/GettyImages; p. 38: Mint Images - Tim Robbins/Mint Images RF/GettyImages; p. 40 (T): Klaus Tiedge/Blend Images/GettyImages; p. 40 (B): nwinter/iStock/Getty Images Plus/GettyImages; p. 43 (Ex 1a): Daniel Allan/Photographer's Choice/GettyImages; p. 43 (Ex 1b): Gary John Norman/Iconica/GettyImages; p. 43 (Ex 1c): Paul Bradbury/Caiaimage/GettyImages; p. 43 (Ex 1d): Dave and Les Jacobs/Lloyd Dobbie/Blend Images/GettyImages; p. 43 (Ex 1e): Hero Images/Hero Images/GettyImages; p. 43 (Ex 1f): BJI/Blue Jean Images/GettyImages; p. 43 (Ex 1g): XiXinXing/GettyImages; p. 43 (Ex 1h): Phil Boorman/Cultura/GettyImages; p. 43 (Ex 1i): Gary John Norman/The Image Bank/GettyImages; p. 43 (Ex 1j): Cultura RM Exclusive/yellowdog/Cultura Exclusive/GettyImages; p. 44 (Ex 2.1): Portra Images/Taxi/GettyImages; p. 44 (Ex 2.2): Paper Boat Creative/DigitalVision/GettyImages; p. 44 (Ex 2.3): Monty Rakusen/Cultura/GettyImages; p. 44 (Ex 2.4): Hero Images/Stone/GettyImages; p. 44 (Ex 2.5): diego_cervo/iStock/Getty Images Plus/GettyImages; p. 44 (Ex 2.6): Caiaimage/Robert Daly/OJO+/GettyImages; p. 45 (TL): Jetta Productions/Iconica/GettyImages; p. 45 (TR): Dana Neely/Stone/GettyImages; p. 45 (BL): Rob Daly/OJO Images/GettyImages; p. 45 (BR): vgajic/E+/GettyImages; p. 46 (T): Hero Images/Hero Images/GettyImages; p. 46 (B): zoranm/E+/GettyImages; p. 47 (T): HAYKIRDI/iStock/Getty Images Plus/GettyImages; p. 47 (B): onepony/iStock/Getty Images Plus/GettyImages; p. 48 (Ex 6.1): Klaus Vedfelt/Taxi/GettyImages; p. 48 (Ex 6.2): Caiaimage/Sam Edwards/Caiaimage/GettyImages; p. 48 (Ex 6.3): Inti St Clair/Blend Images/GettyImages; p. 48 (Ex 6.4): Monty Rakusen/Cultura/GettyImages; p. 48 (Ex 6.5): JGI/Tom Grill/Blend Images/GettyImages; p. 48 (Ex 6.6): Caiaimage/Tom Merton/Caiaimage/GettyImages; p. 49 (Ex 1.1): Rosemary Calvert/Photographer's Choice/GettyImages; p. 49 (Ex 1.2): Bruno Crescia Photography Inc/First Light/GettyImages; p. 49 (Ex 1.3): Roger Dixon/Dorling Kindersley/GettyImages; p. 49 (Ex 1.4): Alexander Bedrin/iStock/Getty Images Plus/GettyImages; p. 49 (Ex 1.5): Kaan Ates/iStock/Getty Images Plus/GettyImages; p. 49 (Ex 1.6): David Marsden/Photolibrary/GettyImages; p. 49 (Ex 1.7): RedHelga/E+/GettyImages; p. 49 (Ex 1.8): rimglow/iStock/Getty Images Plus/GettyImages; p. 49 (Ex 1.9): Suwanmanee99/iStock/Getty Images Plus/GettyImages; p. 49 (Ex 1.10): Creative Crop/DigitalVision/GettyImages; p. 49 (Ex 1.11): Dorling Kindersley/Dorling Kindersley/GettyImages; p. 49 (Ex 1.12): mm88/iStock/Getty Images Plus/GettyImages; p. 49 (Ex 1.13): kbwills/iStock/Getty Images Plus/GettyImages; p. 49 (Ex 1.14): Steve Wisbauer/Photolibrary/GettyImages; p. 49 (Ex 1.15): Tomas_Mina/iStock/Getty Images Plus/GettyImages; p. 49 (Ex 1.16): Freila/iStock/Getty Images Plus/GettyImages; p. 49 (Ex 1.17): Paul Poplis/Photolibrary/GettyImages; p. 49 (Ex 1.18): Dorling Kindersley/Dorling Kindersley/GettyImages; p. 49 (Ex 1.19): Science Photo Library/Science Photo Library/GettyImages; p. 49 (Ex 1.20): Gary Sergraves/Dorling Kindersley/GettyImages; p. 50 (Ex 2.1): Dave King Dorling Kindersley/Dorling Kindersley/GettyImages; p. 50 (Ex 2.2): fcafotodigital/E+/GettyImages; p. 50 (Ex 2.3): Susan Trigg/E+/GettyImages; p. 50 (Ex 2.4): Davies and Starr/The Image Bank/GettyImages; p. 50 (Ex 2.5): Kai Schwabe/StockFood Creative/GettyImages; p. 50 (Ex 2.6): Kevin Summers/Photographer's Choice/GettyImages; p. 50 (Ex 3.1): 109508Liane Riss/GettyImages; p. 51 (T): Digital Vision/Photodisc/GettyImages; p. 51 (B): Lisa Hubbard/Photolibrary/GettyImages; p. 53 (T): MIXA/GettyImages; p. 53 (B): Tom Grill/The Image Bank/GettyImages; p. 54: Jake Curtis/Iconica/GettyImages; p. 55 (Ex 1a): Shell_114/iStock/Getty Images Plus/GettyImages; p. 55 (Ex 1b): C Squared Studios/Photodisc/GettyImages; p. 55 (Ex 1c): Image Source/ Image Source/GettyImages; p. 55 (Ex 1d): inxti/iStock/Getty Images Plus/GettyImages; p. 55 (Ex 1e): skodonnell/E+/GettyImages; p. 55 (Ex 1f): by_nicholas/E+/GettyImages; p. 55 (Ex 1g): koosen/iStock/Getty Images Plus/GettyImages; p. 55 (Ex 1h): Creativ Studio Heinemann/GettyImages; p. 55 (Ex 1i): Lazi & Mellenthin/GettyImages; p. 55 (Ex 1j): stockbymh/iStock/Getty Images Plus/GettyImages; p. 56 (T): John P Kelly/The Image Bank/GettyImages; p. 56 (B): Nicola Tree/The Image Bank/GettyImages; p. 59 (T): Zave Smith/Photolibrary/GettyImages; p. 59 (C): XiXinXing/GettyImages; p. 59 (B): Steve Mcsweeny/Moment/GettyImages; p. 60: Dougal Waters/Taxi/GettyImages; p. 61 (spring): Maria Viola/EyeEm/EyeEm/GettyImages; p. 61 (summer): Dothan Nareswari/EyeEm/EyeEm/GettyImages; p. 61 (fall): Plattform/GettyImages; p. 61 (winter): juliannafunk/iStock/Getty Images Plus/GettyImages; p. 64 (T): VisitBritain/Britain On View/GettyImages; p. 64 (B): GM Visuals/Blend Images/GettyImages; p. 65 (Ex 6.1): T.T./Taxi/GettyImages; p. 65 (Ex 6.2): Jade/Blend Images/GettyImages; p. 65 (Ex 6.3): Hero Images/Hero Images/GettyImages; p. 65 (Ex 6.4): Todor Tsvetkov/E+/GettyImages; p. 65 (Ex 6.5): Hero Images/Hero Images/GettyImages; p. 65 (Ex 6.6): Lucia Lambriex/Taxi/GettyImages; p. 65 (Ex 6.7): Er Creatives Services Ltd/Iconica/GettyImages; p. 65 (Ex 6.8): Susan Chiang/E+/GettyImages; p. 65 (Ex 6.9): PhotoAlto/Teo Lannie/PhotoAlto Agency RF Collections/GettyImages; p. 66 (TL): Maximilian Stock Ltd/Photolibrary/GettyImages; p. 66 (TR): Grafner/iStock/Getty Images Plus/GettyImages; p. 66 (CL): Freek Gout/EyeEm/EyeEm/GettyImages; p. 66 (CR): Vstock LLC/GettyImages; p. 66 (BL): mashabuba/E+/GettyImages; p. 66 (BR): Tom Merton/Caiaimage/GettyImages; p. 70: Nicolas McComber/iStock/Getty Images Plus/GettyImages; p. 73 (bank): Keith Brofsky/Photodisc/GettyImages; p. 73 (coffee shop): Jake Curtis/Iconica/GettyImages; p. 73 (petrol pump): David Lees/Taxi/GettyImages; p. 73 (book store): Jetta Productions/The Image Bank/GettyImages; p. 73 (clothing store): Blend Images - Erik Isakson/Brand X Pictures/GettyImages; p. 73 (post office): Matt Cardy/Stringer/Getty Images Europe/GettyImages; p. 73 (supermarket): Johner Images/GettyImages; p. 73 (pharmacy): Caiaimage/Rafal Rodzoch/Caiaimage/GettyImages; p. 76: Leonardo Patrizi/E+/GettyImages; p. 79 (Ex 1.1): Y.Nakajima/un/ANYONE/amana images/GettyImages; p. 79 (Ex 1.2): John Lund/Marc Romanelli/Blend Images/GettyImages; p. 79 (Ex 1.3): Maskot/Maskot/GettyImages; p. 79 (Ex 1.4): UniversalImagesGroup/Universal Images Group/GettyImages; p. 79 (Ex 1.5): ullstein bild/ullstein bild/GettyImages; p. 79 (Ex 1.6): Geography Photos/Universal Images Group/GettyImages; p. 79 (Ex 1.7): CommerceandCultureAgency/The Image Bank/GettyImages; p. 79 (Ex 1.8): Jose Luis Pelaez Inc/Blend Images/GettyImages; p. 80 (Alisha): Dougal Waters/DigitalVision/GettyImages; p. 80 (Kim): Hero Images/Hero Images/GettyImages; p. 82: ullstein bild/ullstein bild/GettyImages; p. 83: Tetra Images - Chris Hackett/Brand X Pictures/GettyImages; p. 85: Westend61/GettyImages; p. 86 (T): Walter Bibikow/AWL Images/GettyImages; p. 86 (C): Michele Falzone/Photolibrary/GettyImages; p. 86 (B): Takashi Yagihashi/amana images/GettyImages; p. 87 (Ex 3.1): Photos.com/PHOTOS.com>>/Getty Images Plus/GettyImages; p. 87 (Ex 3.2): Piero Pomponi/Hulton Archive/GettyImages; p. 87 (Ex 3.3): KMazur/WireImage/GettyImages; p. 87 (Ex 3.4): Nancy R. Schiff/Hulton Archive/GettyImages; p. 87 (Ex 3.5): API/Gamma-Rapho/GettyImages; p. 87 (Ex 3.6): Jack Mitchell/Archive Photos/GettyImages; p. 88: Christopher Futcher/E+/GettyImages; p. 89: Mel Melcon/Los Angeles Times/GettyImages; p. 90 (T): Kevin Dodge/Blend Images/GettyImages; p. 90 (B): Thomas Barwick/Taxi/GettyImages; p. 91 (L): Stockbyte/Stockbyte/GettyImages; p. 91 (R): nyul/iStock/Getty Images Plus/GettyImages; p. 93: freemixer/iStock/Getty Images Plus/GettyImages; p. 94: Echo/Cultura/GettyImages; p. 95: Stockbyte/Stockbyte/GettyImages; p. 96 (T): Thanks for viewing! www.johnsteelephoto.com/Moment/GettyImages; p. 96 (B): Giordano Cipriani/The Image Bank/GettyImages.

1 Complete the conversations. Use the names in the box.

☐ John ☐ Mr. Garcia ☐ Ms. Baker ☑ Nancy

Hi, _____Nancy_____.

Hello, _____.

It's nice to meet you, _____.

Nice to meet you, too, _____.

2 Complete the conversations. Use *my*, *your*, *his*, or *her*.

1. **A:** Hi. What's _____your_____ name?

   B: _____ name is Lisa. And what's _____ name?

   A: _____ name is James.

2. **A:** What's _____ name?

   B: _____ name is Michael.

   A: And what's _____ name?

   B: _____ name is Susan.

3 Complete the conversations.

1. **A:** Hello, _____Mr._____ Wilson.
   B: _____ morning, David.
      _____ are you?
   A: _____ OK, thank you.

2. **A:** Hi. How are _____ , Mrs. Turner?
   B: I'm just _____ , thank you. How about _____ , _____ Smith?
   A: Pretty _____ , thanks.

3. **A:** How's it _____ , Ken?
   B: Great. _____ are you doing?
   A: Pretty good.

4 Choose the correct responses.

1. A: Hi, Tony.

    B: _____ Hello. _____

       • Hello.

       • It's nice to meet you.

2. A: My name is Ellen Miller.

    B: _____

       • It's Williams.

       • I'm Rob Williams.

3. A: Hello, Carol. How's it going?

    B: _____

       • Fine, thanks.

       • Nice to meet you, too.

4. A: How do you spell your last name?

    B: _____

       • R-O-G-E-R-S.

       • It's Rogers.

5. A: I'm Rich Martinez.

    B: _____

       • Nice to meet you, too.

       • It's nice to meet you.

5 Spell the numbers.

1. 2 _____ two _____

2. 3 _____

3. 8 _____

4. 1 _____

5. 7 _____

6. 10 _____

7. 5 _____

8. 6 _____

9. 0 _____

10. 9 _____

11. 4 _____

6 Write the telephone numbers and email addresses.

1. two-one-two, five-five-five, six-one-one-five   <u>212-555-6115</u>

2. A-M-Y dash L-O-P-E-Z eight-two at C-U-P dot O-R-G   <u>amy-lopez82@cup.org</u>

3. six-oh-four, five-five-five, four-seven-three-one   _____

4. nine-four-nine, five-five-five, three-eight-oh-two   _____

5. B-R-I-A-N dot J-O-H-N-S-O-N zero-three-nine at C-U-P dot O-R-G   _____

6. seven-seven-three, five-five-five, one-seven-seven-nine   _____

7. M-A-R-I-A-B-R-A-D-Y underscore seven at C-U-P dot O-R-G   _____

8. T-I-N-A dash F-O-X underscore nine-five-two at C-U-P dot O-R-G   _____

7 Complete the conversations. Write 'm, 're, or 's.

1. **A:** What <u>'s</u> your name?

   B: I _____ Momoko Sato.

   A: It _____ nice to meet you, Momoko.

2. **A:** Hello. I _____ Josh Brown. I _____ in your English class.

   B: Yes, and you _____ in my math class, too.

3. **A:** What _____ his name?

   B: It _____ Chris Allen.

   A: He _____ in our English class.

   B: You _____ right!

8 Complete the conversations. Use the words in the box.

☐ am	☐ he's	☐ I'm not	☐ it's	☐ you
☐ are	☐ I'm	☐ is	✓ me	☐ you're

1. **Amy:** Excuse _____me_____ . Are
   _____ Alex Walker?

   Carlos: No, _____ .
   _____ over there.

   Amy: Oh, _____ sorry.

2. **Amy:** Excuse me. _____ you
   Alex Walker?

   Alex: Yes, I _____ .

   Amy: Hi, Alex. My name _____
   Amy Clark.

   Alex: Oh, _____ in my English class.

   Amy: That's right. _____ nice to meet you.

   Alex: Nice to meet you, too.

9 Complete the conversation. Use the questions in the box.

☐ What's your name?	☐ And what's your email address?
☐ And how do you spell your last name?	☐ What's your phone number?
✓ Are you Andrea Nelson?	☐ How do you spell your first name?

A: Hi. <u>Are you Andrea Nelson?</u>

B: No, I'm not.

A: Oh, I'm sorry. _____

B: Kerry Moore.

A: _____

B: K-E-R-R-Y.

A: _____

B: M-O-O-R-E.

A: _____

B: It's 618-555-7120.

A: _____

B: It's kmoore19@cup.org.

10 Hello and good-bye!

A Complete the conversations. Use the words in parentheses.

1. A: ___Hi._____

(Hi. / Excuse me.) How are you?

B: I'm fine, thanks.

2. A: _____

(Hello. / Good-bye.)

B: See you tomorrow.

3. A: _____

(Excuse me. / Thank you.) Are you Min-ji Park?

B: Yes, I am. It's nice to meet you.

4. A: _____

(Good evening. / Good night.)

B: Hello.

B Match the pictures with the conversations in part A.

a. ___1___

b. _____

c. _____

d. _____

2 Where are my keys?

1 What are these things?

A What's in the picture? Write the things.

1. _a backpack_
2. _____
3. _____
4. _____
5. _____
6. _____
7. _____
8. _____

B What's in the picture? Write sentences.

1. _This is a backpack._
2. _____
3. _____
4. _____
5. _____
6. _____
7. _____
8. _____

2 Complete the chart with the words in the box.

☑ doors	☐ purses	☐ desks	☐ energy bars
☑ books	☐ umbrellas	☐ hairbrushes	☐ tablets
☑ quizzes	☐ laptops	☐ keys	☐ boxes

/z/		/s/		/ɪz/	
doors	_____	books	_____	quizzes	_____
_____	_____	_____	_____	_____	_____

3 Complete the questions with *this* or *these*. Then answer the questions.

1. A: What's _____this_____ ?
   B: _It's a cell phone._

2. A: What's _____ ?
   B: _____

3. A: What are _____ ?
   B: _____

4. A: What are _____ ?
   B: _____

5. A: What are _____ ?
   B: _____

6. A: What's _____ ?
   B: _____

4 Complete the conversation. Use the words in the box.

| ☐ a | ☐ 's | ☐ this | ☐ they | ☐ you |
| ☐ an | ☑ it's | ☐ these | ☐ they're | ☐ you're |

Clara: Wow! What's this?

Kevin: _____It's_____ a purse.

Clara: Oh, cool. Thank _____ , Kevin.

Kevin: _____ welcome.

Eva: Now open _____ box.

Clara: OK. What _____ this?

Eva: It's _____ tablet case.

Clara: Oh, thank you, Eva. And what are _____ ?

Eva: _____ 're sunglasses.

Clara: Thanks! _____ great!

Laura: Open this, too!

Clara: Oh, it's _____ umbrella. Thanks, Laura!

5 Complete the conversations. Use the answers in the box.

☐ Yes, I am.	☐ Yes, it is.	☐ Yes, they are.	☐ It's
☐ No, I'm not.	☐ No, it's not.	☑ No, they're not.	☐ They're

1. **A:** Are these your books?

   B: _No, they're not._ My books are in my bag.

2. **A:** Excuse me. Is this the math class?

   B: _____ And I'm your teacher.

3. **A:** Is my purse on the chair?

   B: _____ It's under the table.

4. **A:** Where's my laptop?

   B: _____ in your backpack.

5. **A:** Where are your glasses?

   B: _____ in my purse.

6. **A:** Hi. Are you in my math class?

   B: _____ And I'm in your English class, too!

7. **A:** Are these your keys?

   B: _____ Thank you.

8. **A:** Excuse me. Are you Min-soo Cho?

   B: _____ My name is Jin-ho Han. Min-soo isn't in this class.

6 Complete the conversations.

1. **A:** Oh no! Where _____is_____ my tablet?

   B: Is _____ in your backpack?

   A: No, it's _____ .

   B: Hmm. _____ it under your math book?

   A: Yes, it is! Thank you!

2. **A:** _____ this my cell phone?

   B: No, _____ not. It's my cell phone.

   A: Sorry. _____ is my cell phone?

   B: Is _____ in your purse?

   A: Oh, yes, it _____ . Thanks.

3. **A:** Where _____ my keys?

   B: Are _____ in your pocket?

   A: No, they're _____ .

   B: _____ they on the table?

   A: Hmm. Yes, _____ are. Thanks.

4. **A:** _____ my notebook in your backpack?

   B: No, _____ not. Sorry.

   A: Hmm. _____ is my notebook?

   B: _____ it behind your laptop?

   A: Let me see. Yes, it _____ . Thank you!

7 Answer the questions. Use your own information.

1. Are you a teacher?

<u>No, I'm not. I'm a student.</u>

2. Is your name Akiko Nakayama?

_____

3. Is your workbook on your desk?

_____

4. Is your phone number 806-555-0219?

_____

5. Are you in a math class?

_____

8 Complete the sentences. Use the prepositions in the box.

☐ behind   ☑ in   ☐ in front of   ☐ next to   ☐ on   ☐ under

1. The notebook is ____in____ the backpack.

2. The umbrella is _____ the table.

3. The keys are _____ the wallet.

4. The pen is _____ the purse.

5. The laptop is _____ the desk.

6. The wastebasket is _____ the chair.

9 Where are these things?

A Look at the picture. Write questions and answers about the things in parentheses.

1. **A:** <u>Where is the backpack?</u>   (backpack)

   B: <u>It's next to the table.</u>

2. **A:** _____ (books)

   B: _____

3. **A:** _____ (cell phone)

   B: _____

4. **A:** _____ (pens)

   B: _____

5. **A:** _____ (purse)

   B: _____

6. **A:** _____ (sunglasses)

   B: _____

B Write two more questions and answers about the picture.

1. **A:** _____

   B: _____

2. **A:** _____

   B: _____

3 Where are you from?

Cities and countries

A Complete the chart with the languages and nationalities in the box.

☐ Arabic	☐ Japanese
☐ Argentine	☐ Korean
☑ Brazilian	☑ Portuguese
☐ Canadian	☐ South Korean
☐ Colombian	☐ Spanish
☐ Egyptian	☐ Spanish
☐ English	☐ Turkish
☐ French	☐ Turkish
☐ Japanese	

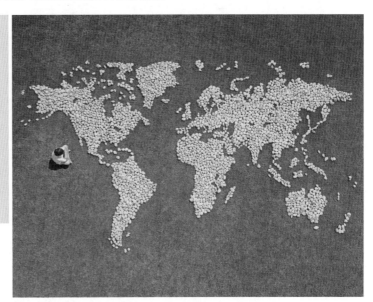

Countries	Nationalities	Languages
Brazil	Brazilian	Portuguese
Colombia	_____	_____
South Korea	_____	_____
Canada	_____	_____
Turkey	_____	_____
Argentina	_____	_____
Japan	_____	_____
Egypt	_____	_____

B Where are these cities? Complete the sentences with the countries in part A.

1. Istanbul and Ankara _are in Turkey._____

2. Bogotá _____

3. Tokyo _____

4. São Paulo and Rio de Janeiro _____

5. Seoul and Daejeon _____

6. Buenos Aires _____

7. Vancouver and Ottawa _____

8. Cairo _____

13

2 Complete the conversations with *am, 'm, are, 're, is,* or *'s.*

1. **A:** _____Are_____ you and your family from New Zealand?

   B: No, we _____ not. We _____ from Australia.

   A: Oh, so you _____ Australian.

   B: Yes, I _____ . I _____ from Melbourne.

2. **A:** _____ Brazil in Central America?

   B: No, it _____ not. It _____ in South America.

   A: Oh. _____ we from Brazil, Dad?

   B: Yes, we _____ . We _____ from Brazil originally, but we _____ here in the U.S. now.

3. **A:** _____ this your wallet?

   B: Yes, it _____ . Thanks.

   A: And _____ these your sunglasses?

   B: Yes, they _____ .

   A: Well, they _____ very nice sunglasses.

   B: Thank you!

4. **A:** _____ your English teacher from the U.S.?

   B: No, she _____ not. She _____ from Canada. Montreal, Canada.

   A: _____ English her first language?

   B: No, it _____ not. Her first language _____ French.

3 Answer the questions.

1. A: Are they from Colombia?

B: _No, they're not. They're from Brazil._

2. A: Is she from India?

B: _____

3. A: Is she from Canada?

B: _____

4. A: Are they in Mexico?

B: _____

5. A: Is he in Bangkok?

B: _____

6. A: Are they in Egypt?

B: _____

4 Spell the numbers.

1. 14 _____fourteen_____
2. 40 _____
3. 60 _____
4. 13 _____
5. 27 _____

6. 102 _____
7. 11 _____
8. 30 _____
9. 18 _____
10. 80 _____

5 Complete the conversations with the correct responses.

1. **A:** Where are they from?

   B: _She's from the U.K., and he's from the U.S._
   - She's Emily Blunt, and he's John Krasinski.
   - She's from the U.K., and he's from the U.S.

2. **A:** Is your first language English?

   B: _____
   - No, it's Japan.
   - No, it's Japanese.

3. **A:** What are they like?

   B: _____
   - They're very serious.
   - They're in Hong Kong.

4. **A:** Who's that?

   B: _____
   - He's the new math teacher.
   - It's my new tablet.

5. **A:** Where are Rahul and his family?

   B: _____
   - They're in the U.S. now.
   - They're from Mumbai.

6. **A:** How old is he now?

   B: _____
   - It's twenty-eight.
   - He's twenty-eight.

7. **A:** What's Marrakech like?

   B: _____
   - It's in Morocco.
   - It's very interesting.

6 Descriptions

A Write sentences about the people in the pictures. Use the words in the box.

☐ funny	☐ serious	☐ talkative
☐ heavy	☐ short	☐ tall
☐ kind	☑ shy	☐ thin

1. Julia is _____shy_____ .

2. Mark and Carlos are
_____ .

3. Brian is _____
and Owen is _____ .

4. Daniel is _____ .

5. Mariko is _____
and Ben is _____ .

6. Ginny is _____ .

7. Dr. Lopez is _____ .

B Answer the questions.

1. Is Ben tall? _Yes, he is._____

2. Is Ginny serious? _____

3. Is Owen thin? _____

4. Is Julia young? _____

5. Are Mark and Carlos male? _____

6. Is Dr. Lopez old? _____

7. Are you kind? _____

8. Are you shy? _____

7 Complete the conversations. Use the words in the boxes.

☐ her   ☐ not   ☑ what's
☐ is   ☐ she's   ☐ where

1. **A:** Annette, ____what's____ your best friend like?

   B: _____ very nice. _____ name is Valentina. I call her Tina.

   A: _____ is she from? _____ she from Spain?

   B: No, she's _____ . She's from Italy.

☐ are   ☐ my   ☐ we're
☐ her   ☐ we   ☐ what's

2. **A:** Toshi, are you and Naomi from Japan?

   B: Yes, _____ are. _____ from Osaka.

   A: _____ your first language?

   B: _____ first language is Japanese, but Naomi's first language is English. _____ parents _____ from New York originally.

8 Answer the questions. Use your own information.

1. Where are you from?

   _____

2. What's your first language?

   _____

3. How are you today?

   _____

4. Where is your teacher from?

   _____

5. What is your teacher like?

   _____

6. What are you like?

   _____

4 Is this coat yours?

1 **Label the clothes. Use the words in the box.**

- ☐ belt
- ☑ jacket
- ☐ high heels
- ☐ sneakers
- ☐ skirt
- ☐ cap
- ☐ T-shirt
- ☐ shorts
- ☐ blouse
- ☐ socks

1. _____jacket_____
2. _____
3. _____
4. _____
5. _____
6. _____
7. _____
8. _____
9. _____
10. _____

2 **What clothes don't belong? Check (✓) the things.**

For work	For home	For cold weather	For warm weather
☐ shirt	☐ T-shirt	☐ boots	☐ swimsuit
✓ shorts	☐ shorts	☐ scarf	☐ T-shirt
☐ tie	☐ suit	☐ shorts	☐ boots
☐ belt	☐ dress	☐ pants	☐ sneakers
✓ swimsuit	☐ jeans	☐ sweater	☐ shorts
☐ shoes	☐ pajamas	☐ gloves	☐ sweater
☐ jacket	☐ coat	☐ T-shirt	☐ cap

3 **What things in your classroom are these colors? Write sentences.**

beige	brown	gray	light blue	pink	red	yellow
black	dark blue	green	orange	purple	white	

1. _My desk is brown._   (brown)
2. _Celia's bag is purple._   (purple)
3. _____ (gray)
4. _____ (white)
5. _____ (red)
6. _____ (green)
7. _____ (black)
8. _____
9. _____
10. _____

4 Whose clothes are these?

Max

Maya

Lisa

A Complete the conversations.

1. A: Whose _scarf is this_ ?

B: _It's Maya's_ .

2. A: Whose _____ ?

B: _____ .

3. A: Whose _____ ?

B: _____ .

4. A: Whose _____ ?

B: _____ .

5. A: Whose _____ ?

B: _____ .

6. A: Whose _____ ?

B: _____ .

B Complete the conversations with the correct words in parentheses.

1. A: _____Whose_____ (Whose / His) T-shirt is this? Is it Ayumi's?

B: No, it's not _____ (her / hers). It's _____ (my / mine).

2. A: Are these _____ (your / yours) jeans?

B: No, they aren't _____ (my / mine) jeans. Let's ask Mohammed. I think they're _____ (his / he's).

3. A: Are these Stephanie's and Jennifer's socks?

B: No, they aren't _____ (their / theirs). They're _____ (your / yours).

A: I don't think so. These socks are white, and _____ (my / mine) are blue.

5 **What season is it? How is the weather? Write two sentences about each picture.**

1. It's fall.
   It's very windy.

2. _____
   _____

3. _____
   _____

4. _____
   _____

5. _____
   _____

6. _____
   _____

6 Waiting for the bus

A Write sentences. Use the words in parentheses.

Steven   Carolina   Sung-min   Allison   Liz   Pablo

1. _Pablo is wearing a tie._ (tie)
2. _Steven and Carolina are wearing boots._ (boots)
3. _____ (T-shirt)
4. _____ (skirt)
5. _____ (dress)
6. _____ (sneakers)
7. _____ (scarf)
8. _____ (hats)

B Correct the false sentences.

1. Sung-min is wearing jeans.

   No, he isn't. / No, he's not. He's wearing shorts.

2. Liz and Pablo are wearing raincoats.

   _____

3. Carolina is wearing a skirt.

   _____

4. Allison is wearing pajamas.

   _____

5. Carolina and Liz are wearing T-shirts.

   _____

6. Steven and Pablo are wearing shorts.

   _____

7 Complete the sentences.

1. My name's Jamie. I'm wearing _____ a T-shirt and shorts. I _____ sneakers, too. It _____ raining, but I _____ a raincoat.

2. It's winter, so Maria _____ high heels – she _____ boots. She _____ a scarf, but she _____ a hat.

3. It's very sunny today, so Richard and Meg _____ sunglasses. It's hot, so Richard _____ shorts and Meg _____ light pants. They _____ sweaters.

4. Ed _____ a suit. He _____ a scarf, but he _____ a tie. He _____ shoes and socks. It's very windy.

8 Complete these sentences with and, but, or so.

1. He's wearing jeans and sneakers, _____and_____ he's wearing a T-shirt.

2. It's very cold outside, _____ I'm not wearing a coat.

3. Her skirt is blue, _____ her blouse is blue, too.

4. It's raining, _____ I need an umbrella.

5. He's wearing an expensive suit, _____ he's wearing sneakers.

6. It's summer and it's very sunny, _____ it's hot.

What time is it?

1 Write each sentence a different way.

1. It's midnight. _It's twelve o'clock at night._

2. It's 7:00 A.M. _____

3. It's 2:45 P.M. _____

4. It's 9:20 A.M. _____

5. It's 6:15 P.M. _____

6. It's 11:00 P.M. _____

7. It's 3:30 A.M. _____

8. It's 12:00 P.M. _____

2 What time is it in each city? Write the time in two different ways.

1. _It's 10:00 A.M. in Seattle._

  It's ten o'clock in the morning.

2. _____

_____

3. _____

_____

4. _____

_____

5. _____

_____

6. _____

_____

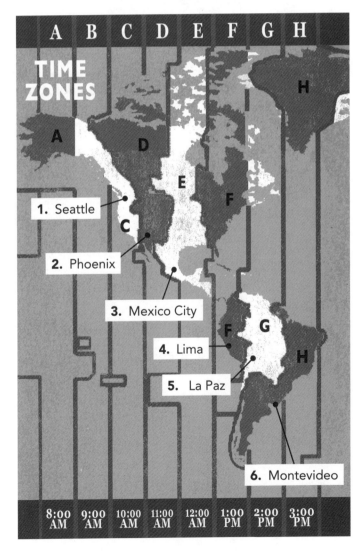

TIME ZONES

A B C D E F G H

A

D

E

F

H

1. Seattle

C

2. Phoenix

3. Mexico City

F   G

4. Lima

H

5. La Paz

6. Montevideo

| 8:00 AM | 9:00 AM | 10:00 AM | 11:00 AM | 12:00 AM | 1:00 PM | 2:00 PM | 3:00 PM |

3 What time is it? Use the sentences in the box.

☑ It's a quarter after five.	☐ It's nine-oh-three.
☐ It's a quarter to two.	☐ It's ten after eight.
☐ It's four-thirty.	☐ It's twelve o'clock.

1. It's a quarter after five.   **2.** _____   **3.** _____

4. _____   **5.** _____   **6.** _____

4 Complete the sentences. Write each time a different way.

1. It's six in the morning. It's six _____A.M._____

2. It's 10:00 P.M. It's ten at _____ .

3. It's 5:15. It's five- _____ .

4. It's 7:00 P.M. It's seven in the _____ .

5. It's 4:30. It's four- _____ .

6. It's 8:00 A.M. It's eight in the _____ .

7. It's twelve P.M. It's _____ .

8. It's 2:00 P.M. It's two in the _____ .

9. It's twelve A.M. It's _____ .

10. It's 6:45. It's a _____ to seven.

11. It's 11:15. It's a quarter _____ eleven.

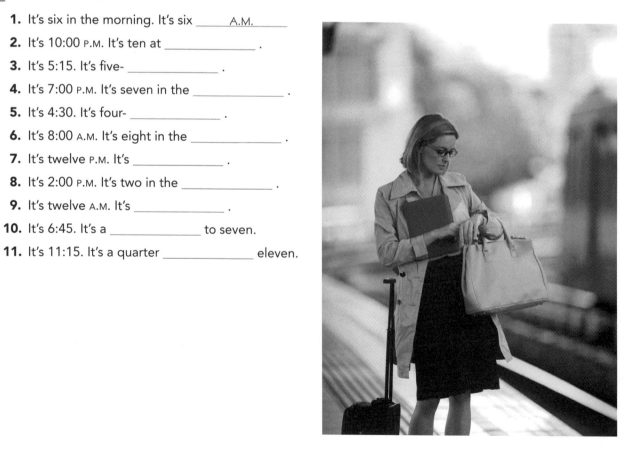

5 | What are these people doing? Write sentences. Use the words in the box.

- [ ] call a friend
- [x] make coffee
- [ ] take a walk
- [ ] drive
- [ ] ride a bike
- [ ] watch a movie
- [ ] have breakfast
- [ ] shop
- [ ] work

1. He's making coffee.
2. _____
3. _____

4. _____
5. _____
6. _____

7. _____
8. _____
9. _____

6 Answer these questions.

1. Is Salma sleeping?

No, she's not. She's studying.

2. Are Richard and Laura playing tennis?

No, they're not. They're dancing.

3. Is Charles visiting friends?

_____

4. Is Jerry eating dinner?

_____

5. Are Mary and Jennifer checking their messages?

_____

6. Is Carol listening to music?

_____

7. Is Kevin driving?

_____

8. Are the friends watching a movie?

_____

7 **Write questions about these people. Use the words in parentheses.
Then answer the questions.**

1. **A:** _Is Min wearing jeans?_
   (Min / wear jeans)

   B: _No, she's not. She's wearing a dress._

2. **A:** _____
   (Bob / drink soda)

   B: _____

3. **A:** _____
   (Jason and Beth / watch a movie)

   B: _____

4. **A:** _____
   (Adriana / wear jeans)

   B: _____

5. **A:** _____
   (Amy and Gabriela / chat online)

   B: _____

6. **A:** _____
   (Daniel / talk to Adriana)

   B: _____

7. **A:** _____
   (Bob / wear shorts)

   B: _____

8. **A:** _____
   (Min / talk on the phone)

   B: _____

8 Write questions and answers. Use *What* + *doing* and the words in parentheses.

1. **A:** _What is Linda doing?_ (Linda)
   B: _She's checking her messages._ (check her messages)

2. **A:** _What are you and Akira doing?_ (you and Akira)
   B: _We're eating lunch._ (eat lunch)

3. **A:** _____ (Tom and Donna)
   B: _____ (visit friends)

4. **A:** _____ (Sandra)
   B: _____ (get up)

5. **A:** _____ (you and Isabella)
   B: _____ (ride bikes)

6. **A:** _____ (Diego and Patricia)
   B: _____ (work)

7. **A:** _____ (Tim)
   B: _____ (listen to music)

8. **A:** _____ (you)
   B: _____ (study English)

9. **A:** _____ (Sonya and Annie)
   B: _____ (have dinner)

10. **A:** _____ (I)
    B: _____ (finish this exercise)

9 What are you doing? What are your friends doing? Write sentences.

1. _____
   _____

2. _____
   _____

3. _____
   _____

4. _____
   _____

5. _____
   _____

6. _____
   _____

6 I ride my bike to school.

1 Family

A Angela is talking about her family. Complete the sentences with the words in the box.

☐ brother	☐ father	☑ parents	☐ wife	☐ children
☐ husband	☐ sister	☐ daughters	☐ mother	☐ son

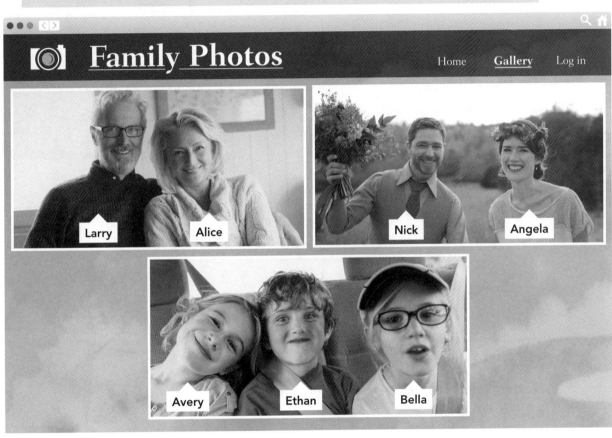

Family Photos   Home   **Gallery**   Log in

Larry   Alice

Nick   Angela

Avery   Ethan   Bella

1. Alice and Larry are my ____parents____ . Alice is my _____ ,
   and Larry is my _____ .

2. Nick is my _____ . I'm his _____ .

3. Ethan, Avery, and Bella are our _____ . Avery and Bella are our _____ , and
   Ethan is our _____ . Avery is Bella's _____ , and Ethan is her _____ .

B Write four sentences about your family.

1. _____
2. _____
3. _____
4. _____

2 Complete the conversation with the correct words in parentheses.

Christine: So, do you live downtown, Sarah?

Sarah: Yes, I _____live_____ with my brother.
(live / lives)

He _____ an apartment near here.
(have / has)

Christine: Oh, so you _____ to work.
(walk / walks)

Sarah: Actually, I _____ walk to work in
(don't / doesn't)

the morning. I _____ the bus to work,
(take / takes)

and then I _____ home at night.
(walk / walks)

What about you?

Christine: Well, my husband and I _____ a house
(have / has)

in the suburbs now, so I _____ to work.
(drive / drives)

My husband doesn't _____ downtown.
(work / works)

He _____ in the suburbs near our house,
(work / works)

so he _____ to work by bus.
(go / goes)

3 Third-person singular –s endings

A Write the third-person singular forms of these verbs.

1. dance ____dances____

2. do ____does____

3. go _____

4. have _____

5. live _____

6. ride _____

7. sleep _____

8. study _____

9. take _____

10. use _____

11. walk _____

12. watch _____

B Practice the words in part A. Then add them to the chart.

s = /s/	s = /z/	(e)s = /ɪz/	irregular
_____	_____	___dances___	___does___
_____	_____	_____	_____
_____	_____	_____	_____

4 True or false?

A Are these sentences true for you? Check (✓) True or False.

	True	False
1. I ride the bus to school.	☐	☐
2. I have a car.	☐	☐
3. I live in the suburbs.	☐	☐
4. I have brothers / a brother.	☐	☐
5. I do my homework at the library.	☐	☐
6. I do my homework alone.	☐	☐
7. I live in a house.	☐	☐
8. I have sisters / a sister.	☐	☐
9. I live with my parents.	☐	☐
10. I work in an office.	☐	☐

B Correct the false statements in part A.

I don't ride the bus to school. I ride my bike to school.

_____
_____
_____
_____
_____
_____
_____
_____
_____
_____
_____
_____
_____
_____
_____
_____

5 Write about Daniela's weekly schedule. Use the words in parentheses.

	Monday	Tuesday	Wednesday	Thursday	Friday
7:00 A.M.	get up ————————————————————————→				
8:00 A.M.	go to work ————————————————————————→				
9:00 A.M.					
10:00 A.M.					
11:00 A.M.	have lunch ————————————————————————→				
12:00 P.M.					
1:00 P.M.					
2:00 P.M.	take a walk ————————————————————————→				
3:00 P.M.					
4:00 P.M.					
5:00 P.M.	finish work ————————————————————————→				
6:00 P.M.	play basketball	go to class	eat dinner with my family	go to class	watch a movie

1. _She gets up at 7:00 every day._ (7:00)
2. _____ (8:00)
3. _____ (11:00)
4. _____ (2:00)
5. _____ (5:00)
6. _____ (6:00 / Mondays)
7. _____ (6:00 / Tuesdays and Thursdays)
8. _____ (6:00 / Fridays)

6 Write something you do and something you don't do on each day.
Use the phrases in the box or your own information.

check email	exercise	have dinner late	sleep late
drive a car	get up early	play video games	talk on the phone
eat breakfast	go to school	see my friends	watch a movie

1. Monday _I get up early on Mondays. I don't sleep late on Mondays._
2. Tuesday _____
3. Wednesday _____
4. Thursday _____
5. Friday _____
6. Saturday _____
7. Sunday _____

7 **Complete these conversations with *at*, *in*, or *on*. (If you don't need a preposition, write Ø.)**

1. **A:** Do you go to bed ___Ø___ late ___on___ weekends?

   B: Yes, I do. I go to bed _____ midnight. But I go to bed _____ early _____ weekdays.

2. **A:** Do you study _____ the afternoon?

   B: No, I study _____ the morning _____ weekends, and I study _____ the evening _____ Mondays and Wednesdays.

3. **A:** What time do you get up _____ the morning _____ weekdays?

   B: I get up _____ 6:00 _____ every day.

4. **A:** Do you have English class _____ the morning?

   B: No, I have English _____ 3:30 _____ the afternoon _____ Tuesdays and Thursdays. _____ Mondays, Wednesdays, and Fridays, our class is _____ 5:00.

8 **Write questions to complete the conversations.**

1. **A:** *Do you live alone?*

   B: No, I don't live alone. I live with my mom and dad.

2. **A:** _____

   B: Yes, my family and I watch television in the afternoon.

3. **A:** _____

   B: Yes, I get up early on Fridays.

   A: _____

   B: I get up at 5:30.

4. **A:** _____

   B: No, my sister doesn't drive to work.

   A: _____

   B: No, she doesn't take the bus. She takes the train.

5. **A:** _____

   B: No, my dad doesn't work on weekends.

   A: _____

   B: He works on weekdays.

6. **A:** _____

   B: Yes, my mom works in the city. She's a restaurant manager.

   A: _____

   B: No, she doesn't use public transportation. She drives to work.

7. **A:** _____

   B: Yes, we have a big lunch on Sundays.

   A: _____

   B: We have lunch at 1:00.

9 Write each sentence a different way. Use the sentences in the box.

☐ He goes to work before noon.	☐ She doesn't get up early on Sundays.
☐ I don't work far from here.	☐ We don't live in the suburbs.
☑ Kimberly is Dan's wife.	☐ We take the bus, the train, or the subway.

1. Dan is Kimberly's husband.

Kimberly is Dan's wife.

2. We have an apartment in the city.

_____

3. We use public transportation.

_____

4. He goes to work in the morning.

_____

5. My office is near here.

_____

6. She sleeps late on Sundays.

_____

10 Answer the questions about your schedule.

1. What do you do on weekdays?

_____

2. What do you do on weekends?

_____

3. What do you do on Friday nights?

_____

4. What do you do on Sunday mornings?

_____

Does it have a view?

1 Label the parts of the house.

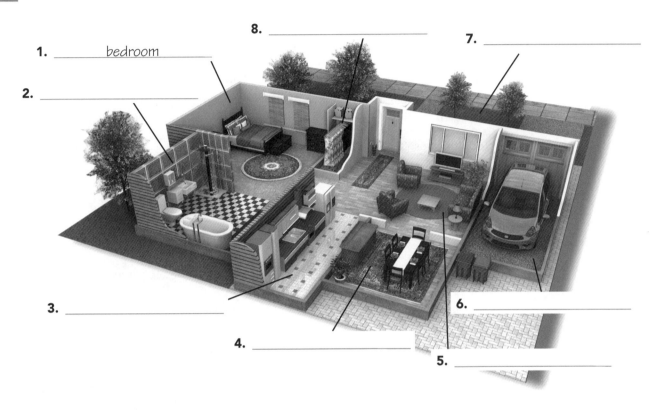

8. _____

7. _____

1. _____bedroom_____

2. _____

3. _____

4. _____

5. _____

6. _____

2 Complete the conversation. Use the sentences in the box.

☐ No, I don't. I live with my sisters.	☐ Yes, it has three bedrooms.
☑ No, I live in an apartment.	☐ Yes, it has a great view of the city.

Ji-hye: Do you live in a house, Fernanda?

Fernanda: _No, I live in an apartment._

Ji-hye: Well, is it very big?

Fernanda: _____

Ji-hye: Does it have a view?

Fernanda: _____

Ji-hye: Oh, that's great! And do you live alone?

Fernanda: _____

3 Complete the conversation with the correct words in parentheses.

Al: _____Do_____ you _____ near here, Brandon?
(Do / Does)   (live / lives)

Brandon: Yes, I _____ . My wife and I _____ on Main Street.
(do / does)   (live / lives)

Al: Oh, do you _____ in an apartment?
(live / lives)

Brandon: No, we _____ . We _____ a house.
(don't / doesn't)   (have / has)

Al: Oh, great! _____ you _____ children?
(Do / Does)   (have / has)

Brandon: No, we _____ .
(don't / doesn't)

But my mother _____ with us.
(live / lives)

Al: Really? Does she do a lot of work at home?

Brandon: Yes, she _____ .
(do / does)

In fact, she _____ dinner every night!
(cook / cooks)

Al: You're lucky! I _____ alone,
(live / lives)

and I _____ my own dinner.
(cook / cooks)

4 Answer these questions with your information. Use short answers.

1. Do you live in a house?   _Yes, I do. / No, I don't._

2. Do you have a garage?   _____

3. Do you live with your family?   _____

4. Does your city or town have a park?   _____

5. Does your teacher have a car?   _____

6. Do you and your classmates speak English?   _____

7. Do you and your classmates study together?   _____

8. Does your classroom have a view?   _____

9. Does your school have a lobby?   _____

10. Does your city or town have a subway?   _____

5 What furniture do they have?

A Answer the questions about the pictures.

1. **A:** Do they have a rug?
   B: _Yes, they do._
2. **A:** Do they need a table?
   B: _____
3. **A:** Do they have chairs?
   B: _____
4. **A:** Do they need a dresser?
   B: _____
5. **A:** Do they have a mirror?
   B: _____
6. **A:** Do they have curtains?
   B: _____

7. **A:** Does he have a bookcase?
   B: _____
8. **A:** Does he need curtains?
   B: _____
9. **A:** Does he need a sofa?
   B: _____
10. **A:** Does he have a chair?
    B: _____
11. **A:** Does he have a lamp?
    B: _____
12. **A:** Does he need pictures?
    B: _____

B What furniture do you have? What furniture do you need? Write four sentences.

1. _____
_____
2. _____
_____
3. _____
_____
4. _____
_____

6 | Complete the description with 's, are, or aren't.

In Martin's apartment, there's _____ a big living room. There _____ two bedrooms and two bathrooms. There _____ no elevator, but there _____ stairs. He has a lot of books, so there _____ bookcases in the living room and bedrooms. There _____ any chairs in the kitchen, but there _____ a big table with chairs in the dining room. There _____ no coffee maker in the kitchen, but there _____ a microwave oven. There _____ two televisions in Martin's apartment – there _____ one television in the living room, and there _____ one television in the bedroom.

7 | Answer these questions with information about your home. Use the phrases in the box.

there are no . . .	there isn't a . . .
there are some . . .	there's a . . .
there aren't any . . .	there's no . . .

1. Does your kitchen have a microwave?

   Yes, there's a microwave in my kitchen.

   No, there isn't a microwave. / No, there's no microwave.

2. Does your kitchen have a stove?

   _____

3. Do you have a sofa in your living room?

   _____

4. Do you have bookcases in your living room?

   _____

5. Does your bathroom have a clock?

   _____

6. Do you have pictures in your bedroom?

   _____

7. Does your bedroom have a closet?

   _____

8 What's wrong with this house?

A Write sentences about the house. Use *there* and the words in parentheses.

1. __There is no stove in the kitchen. / There isn't a stove in the kitchen.__ (stove / kitchen)
2. _____ (chairs / dining room)
3. _____ (stove / living room)
4. _____ (refrigerator / bedroom)
5. _____ (bed / bedroom)
6. _____ (armchairs / bathroom)
7. _____ (bed / kitchen)
8. _____ (bookcases / living room)

B Write four more sentences about the house.

1. _____
2. _____
3. _____
4. _____

9 Choose the correct responses.

1. A: My apartment has a view of the park.

    B: _You're lucky._

- Guess what!
- You're lucky.

2. A: Do you need living room furniture?

    B: _____

- Yes, I do. I need a sofa and a coffee table.
- No, I don't. I need a sofa and a coffee table.

3. A: I really need a new desk.

    B: _____

- So let's go shopping this weekend.
- That's great!

4. A: Do you have chairs in your kitchen?

    B: _____

- Yes, I do. I need six chairs.
- Yes, I do. I have six chairs.

10 Draw a picture of your home. Then write a description. Use the questions in the box for ideas.

Do you live in a house or an apartment?	What rooms does your home have?
What furniture do you have?	Who lives with you?

_____

_____

_____

_____

Where do you work?

1 Match these jobs with the correct pictures.

1. lawyer __c__

2. photographer _____

3. bellhop _____

4. police officer _____

5. pilot _____

6. nurse _____

7. server _____

8. salesperson _____

9. cashier _____

10. front desk clerk _____

2 What do these people do? Write three sentences about each person. Use the phrases in the box and your own ideas.

handle food	help people	wear a uniform	work inside
handle money	sit / stand all day	work hard	work outside

1. _She's a doctor._
   She helps people.
   She works in a hospital.

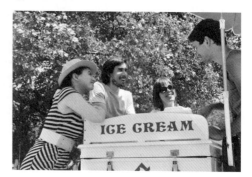

2. _____
   _____
   _____

3. _____
   _____
   _____

4. _____
   _____
   _____

5. _____
   _____
   _____

6. _____
   _____
   _____

3 **Complete the questions in these conversations.**

 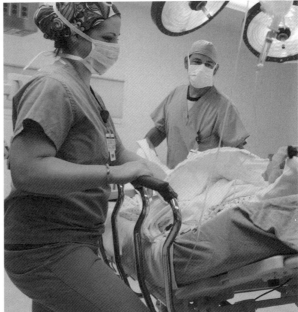

1. A: Where _does your sister work_ ?

   B: My sister? She works in a restaurant.

   A: What _does she do_ ?

   B: She works in the kitchen. She's a chef.

2. A: What _____ ?

   B: Victoria and Jon are nurses. And they work together, too.

   A: Where _____ ?

   B: At Springfield Hospital.

3. A: Where _____ ?

   B: My daughter works in an office.

   A: What _____ ?

   B: She's an accountant.

4. A: What _____ ?

   B: Don and I? We're software engineers.

   A: How _____ ?

   B: We like it a lot!

4 Complete the conversations.

1. **A:** _____Do_____ you _____have_____ a job?

   B: Yes, I _____ .

   A: Oh, what _____ you _____ ?

   B: I _____ a graphic designer.

   A: Where _____ you _____ ?

   B: I _____ at home.

   A: Oh, wow! How _____ you _____ your job?

   B: I really _____ it. It's a great job!

   A: What time _____ you start work?

   B: I _____ work at 8:00 A.M., and I _____ at 3:00 P.M.

2. **A:** My brother _____ a new job.

   B: Really? Where _____ he _____ ?

   A: He _____ at the Town Center Mall.

   B: What _____ he _____ there?

   A: He _____ a security guard.

   B: How _____ he _____ his job?

   A: Oh, I guess he _____ it.

   B: What time _____ he _____ work?

   A: He _____ work at 10:00 A.M., and he _____ at 6:00 P.M.

5 Exciting or boring?

A Match the adjectives.

1. _d_ exciting
2. _____ easy
3. _____ relaxing
4. _____ safe

a. not stressful
b. not difficult
c. not dangerous
d. not boring

B Write each sentence two different ways.

1. An actor's job is exciting.
   An actor has an exciting job.
   An actor doesn't have a boring job.

2. A security guard has a boring job.
   _____
   _____

3. Paul's job is dangerous.
   _____
   _____

4. A front desk clerk's job is stressful.
   _____
   _____

5. Amanda has a small apartment.
   _____
   _____

6. Cristina's house is big.
   _____
   _____

7. Brenda has a talkative brother.
   _____
   _____

8. My job is easy.
   _____
   _____

6 Write sentences with your opinion about each job.

athlete

mechanic

artist

scientist

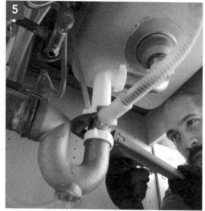

plumber

reporter

1. <u>An athlete has an exciting job. / An athlete's job isn't boring.</u>
2. _____
3. _____
4. _____
5. _____
6. _____

7 Imagine you have a dream job. Write a description. Use the questions in the box for ideas.

What's the job?	What do you do, exactly?
Where do you work?	What's the job like? (Is it dangerous, relaxing, or . . . ?)

_____

_____

_____

_____